PRIVACY IN THE DIGITAL AGE

Digital Communication and Personal Data

Editors:

Nil Çokluk – Nurat Kara

LITERATURK
academia

Privacy in the Digital Age

© LITERATÜRK academia 399
Review-Research 375

October 2022

Editor: **Muzaffer YILMAZ**
Chief Editor: **İsmail ÇALIŞKAN**

ISBN 978-625-7606-79-0

Republic of Turkey
Ministry of Culture and Tourism
Publisher Certificate Number: **16195**

Book Cover Design: DIZGIMIZANPAJ.com
Prepress Preparation: **Mehmet ATEŞ**
meh_ates@hotmail.com

LIBRARY CARD CATALOGUE
- Cataloging in Publication Data (CIP) -

ÇOKLUK / KARA, Nil / Nurat
Privacy in the Digital Age

KEY CONCEPTS
1. Digital communication, 2. Data Security, 3. Privacy, 4. Cyber security, 5. IT law, 6. Digital Literacy

LITERATÜRK academia ", is a Nüve Culture Center Association
www.literaturkacademia.com

 / Nkmliteraturk

M. Muzaffer Cad. Rampalı Çarşı Alt Kat No: 35-36-41   Ул. М. Музаффер, рынок Рампалы, нижний этаж № 35-36-41
Meram / KONYA Tel: 0.332.352 23 03 Fax: 0.332.342 42 96   Мерам, КОНЬЯ, тел.: +90 332 352 23 03, факс: +90 332 342 42 96

Dağıtım: **MIKYAS BOOK PUBLICATION DISTRIBUTION**   **CENTRAL ASIA REPRESENTATIVE:**
Alemdar Mah. Güzel Sanatlar Sk. No: 2/A   Mikrareyon Kok Jar/23   Bishkek / KYRGYSZTAN
Cağaloğlu / ISTANBUL Telefaks +90 212 528 95 28   Tel: +996 700 13 50 00   -   Telefaks: + 996 552 13 50 00
Распространение: **MIKYAS KITAP YAYIN DAGITIM**   **ОФИС В ЦЕНТРАЛЬНОЙ АЗИИ:**
Алемдар Мах. Изобразительное искусство Ск. №: 2/A   Микрорайон Кок Жар/23   Бишкек / КЫРГЫЗСТАН
Джагалоглу / СТАМБУЛ Телефакс +90 212 528 95 28   Тел.: +996 700 13 50 00 – Телефакс: +996 552 13 50 00

PRIVACY IN THE DIGITAL AGE
Digital Communication and Personal Data

Editors:
Nil Çokluk – Nurat Kara

FOREWORD

The vast amount of data that people provide through technology brings new opportunities, but also creates new dilemmas. One of these dilemmas is the issue of privacy. With the development of digital technologies day by day, data pieces have been processed and people's behaviors have become traceable and identifiable. All digital traces of individuals communicating in digital environments can be collected, stored, reprocessed and used. This situation necessitated rethinking the issues of data security and privacy. Users need to be conscious of digital literacy in order to regulate data security and privacy in digital environments. In addition, how or what conditions the data can be collected and used should be subject to legal regulations.

This study on data security and privacy, which are among the main issues with the spread of digital communication, includes articles by different academicians. The book, which includes great effort, has emerged as the product of a collective effort. In this context, we would like to thank all the authors who supported the publication of the book with their articles. We are also grateful to Mahmut Demir for his support. In addition, thanks to Merve Özdemir, Sezgin Savaş and Yıldıray Kesgin, who contributed to the evaluation of the articles. Endless thanks to İsmail Çalışkan, who stood by us and supported us in all the difficulties we encountered during the publishing process.

The book is prepared with the perspective of computer science and communication. The book, which has a multidisciplinary, interdisciplinary and transdisciplinary nature, offers limited information on the subject. Due to the rapid technological development, it is necessary to carry out up-to-date studies on this subject. We hope the book will guide experts, academicians, students and researchers who want to work on this subject. In addition, the book aims to contribute to the building of conscious individuals and society on digital communication, new technologies, data security and privacy. The authors put forward their ideas for the conscious individual and a digital literate society. Hoping to contribute to the construction of a safe and conscious society….

Nil ÇOKLUK
Nurat KARA
September 2022

CONTENTS

HAS PRIVACY ENDED?
AN EVALUATION OF DIGITAL COMMUNICATION
AND DATA SECURITY

*Nil ÇOKLUK**

INTRODUCTION

After the Industrial Revolution took place in the 19th century, the growth in industry, developments in transportation and communication brought social, economic and political transformations. Postman (2006) stated that in addition to these transformations in the 20th century, there was an information explosion with technological developments. As the methods of controlling information become compulsory and more comprehensive, the number of people and institutions implementing these methods has increased. Thus, the information produced by the bureaucracy has increased (Postman, 2006, p. 102). Neil Postman, in his work titled "Technopoly: The New World Order", talks about the necessity of every culture to sit at the negotiating table with technology. According to Postman, it is necessary to see what technology gains and loses (Postman, 2006, p. 16). While technology makes daily life easier, it also reveals the violation of privacy due to negative situations such as surveillance and recording the individual's entire life

Personal data is violated by recording digital traces of contracts that users unwittingly approve. Digital traces of users are collected from factors such as which website they browse, what

* Assistant Professor, Hatay Mustafa Kemal University, Communication Faculty, Public Relations and Publicty Department, nilcokluk@gmail.com

content they read and watch, where and when they are online, and which device they use. All traces left by users and their interactions are used as data to transform into information. In addition to digital traces, personal data can be collected from traffic cameras, home monitoring systems, smart cities, GPS, wearable electronic devices, sensory systems, cards and health monitoring devices. While recording data brings great improvements in government planning, city management, traffic control, public safety, health efficiency, economic development, it poses a significant risk to personal privacy (Tan & Privot, 2015, p. 860).

Addressing the destruction caused by scientific and technological developments in his work titled Civilization and Its Discontents, Freud (1961) emphasizes that the developments have led to undesirable results. Internet technology, which is the carrier of all kinds of information and content, offers the opportunity to reach the masses instantly. In addition, it has multimedia, easy storage and archiving features (Bostancı, 2015, p. 8). In the digital environment, social media platforms allow users to produce visual, auditory and literary content with their own friendship connections. In addition, these platforms provide an environment in which other users participate by watching the content produced by them in a passive position (Savaş, 2021, p. 166). While this provides great convenience in daily life, it puts privacy at risk. The traces left by individuals in digital environments are collected and their data is stored. Data stored over digital media can be used in a wide variety of ways by many different fields (Savaş, 2021, p. 166).

Digital communication is a matter of how individuals, technology developers, policy makers, service providers define identity. In addition, digital communication is directly linked to the way these actors redefine privacy in daily life. Therefore focusing on identity and privacy in digital environments is important to ensure that social networks and e-services are reliable (Cullen & Reilly, 2008). Focusing on identity and privacy in the digital environment provides the opportunity to support privacy policies and develop the conscious and responsible use of e-services (Wessels, 2012, p. 2). Privacy is related to a structure that can develop, reveal, monitor or record information and human behavior, thoughts, beliefs or emotions that are beyond the field of view of others (Allen, 1988, p. 15). Information about personal interests, political views, sexual orientation, race, religion, health, finance, social connections and friends are related to privacy (Tan & Privot, 2015, p. 860).

This study aims to improve understanding of digital communication, data security and privacy. The study deals with the social and economic relations that have changed as a result of social, economic and political transformations in the digital environment in the context of privacy and data security. The study discusses what are the most effective policies for personal data breach resulting from storing and reusing digital traces of individuals. The study basically seeks answers to the questions "What are the transformations experienced as a result of the digitalization of communication in the information age", "What are the problems that will arise as a result of digital platforms storing personal data", "What factors should be considered in order to protect personal data and privacy". In this way, it tries to explain the data security and privacy issues that arise as a result of the digitalization of communication.

The digital age, in which digital communication becomes widespread, is characterized by the increasing role of information and technologies in people's lives. The increasing role of technology in daily life raises the question of how to ensure user privacy. Due to the global use of technology, it is an important issue by whom and how to protect personal data in the global network area. In this context, the elements that form the basis for the development of the information society based on the technologies of the digital age are explained in the study. In addition, the personal data breach and privacy problem that arising from recording the digital traces left by users in digital environments are addressed. The study, which describes the role of information technologies in processing personal data, suggests that adequate data protection should be ensured, users' awareness of digital literacy should be raised, information security principles should be implemented and the requirements of the legal framework regarding the protection of personal data should be met.

The Information Age and the Digitization of Communication

Technological developments bring about some developments and changes in the field of communication, as in many other fields in the world. As a result of technological developments, the communication process has become independent of time and space. With this situation, it can be said that the concept of virtual communication has become important. In today's societies, individuals can share and interact with each other through virtual environments, regardless of time and space (Özcan & Savaş, 2021, p. 121). This is related to the rapid realization of the changes in the 21st century. With the frequent use of technological innovations in daily life, concepts such as information society, network society and information society have begun to be used frequently. With the emergence of some radical innovations in the field of technology, knowledge has become an important element. The fact that technological developments allow to process personal information has created an information society with its own characteristics.

Scientists have classified the ages as the product of a scientific effort. While Arnold Toynbee used the term Industrial Revolution, Daniel Bell used the term Post Industrial Revolution. C. S. Peirce called the 19th century the Railway Age, while Oswald Spengler spoke of the Age of Machine Techniques. Lewis Mumford made a classification as pre-technical, old technique, and new technique. Jose Ortega y Gasset made a parallel distinction with technological development. Gasset has classified the age of technology that happened by chance, the age of technology created by craftsmen, and the age of technology created by technical staff. Walter Ong distinguished between oral, written, and topographic and electronic culture (Postman, 2006, p. 34). McLuhan used the terms Gutenberg Age and the Electronic Communication Age that replaced it Alvin Toffler used the concept of the third wave for the electronics, information and information society. Marshall McLuhan used the concept of global village in 1963. With this usage, McLuhan (1989) emphasized the physical shrinkage of the world and the acceleration and intensification of world-scale interaction in parallel with the development of communication and communication technology.

The information age did not begin with computers. The beginning of the information age began with the discovery of the printing press in the first years of the 16th century (Postman, 2006, p. 76). The printing press and the book spread over a wide area with the development of the printing press. With the printing press, a society has emerged where information becomes standardized and reproducible. With the development and spread of new technologies, communication between people and societies has increased. In the 19th century, the communication revolution took place with the acceleration of the development of technology. Considering the developments that led to the communication revolution; 1830s photography and telegraph, 1840s rotary (a type of printing press), 1866 transatlantic cable, 1876 telephone, film and 1895 wireless telegraph (Postman, 2006, p. 55) radio in the same year, television in 1923 and computer in 1946, 1950s internet. As a result of these developments, we have entered the information age. As a result of the developments experienced, it has become an important power to keep data, information and information with the digitalization of communication and daily life practices.

The concept of information society is a social structure in which all areas of life are increasingly occupied by information and communication technology. In the information society, communication itself has become a productive force (Seubert & Becker, 2019, p. 2). Information society; As a result of the information explosion that marked the recent era, it is a social structure in which the basic production factor is information, and the processing and storage of information is based on computer and communication technologies. Daniel Bell, who used the concept of post-industrial society, was one of the first thinkers to use the concept of the information society. Bell first mentioned the concept of information society in his work The Coming of Post Industrial Society (2018). Intellectual technology is rising in this society. Information has become a strategically important element in the information society where computer technologies have gained importance. In the information age, information is constantly produced, spread and accumulated (Kara, 2021, p. 313). Who owns the information and the way it is used are as important as the information produced. The power of thought and reason has gained importance in the information society. In addition, with the development of technology, communication has become faster and easier. This situation has enabled communication and communication to gain a global dimension. Access to information has gained speed thanks to information networks and databases. Education has become individual and continuous. Technological opportunities have emerged that will enable the production and processing of new information continuously.

With the development of information technologies, digitalization has increased. Digitization can be defined as the process of transferring the analogue world to the digital environment. Digitalization has allowed society to store more information and process this information faster (Mai, 2016, p. 193). In addition, with digitalization, communication has started to take place through technology. The extensive digitization of the communication infrastructure has led to the commodification of personal data (Seubert & Becker, 2019, p. 2). With big data methods, personal data has become easily stored, processed and used. Arslantaş-Toktaş et al. (2012, p. 15) say that with technological developments, systematically recording every stage of social life is perceived as a natural process. Users voluntarily request to be included in the system where all data is added. This situation necessitates the discussion of data security and privacy issues.

Digital Communication and Data Security

In the information age, digital communication comes to the fore. With the digitalization of communication, recording the traces left by users in digital environments has revealed the problem of data security and privacy. The political scandals that emerged with Snowden's disclosure of large amounts of data and Cambridge Analytica's unauthorized use of personal data in electoral work brought data security and privacy issues to the fore. Recently, with the rapid development of communication technologies and digital storage and transfer of personal data, data security and privacy have become issues that need to be regulated legally.

Since the 1970s, the capacity of modern information and communication technologies to access, store and share personal information has increased. The information collected about users in daily life and the voluntary public sharing of "private" behaviors on social media complicates the issue of privacy in the digital age (Bajpai & Weber, 2017, p. 224). Data privacy is about users having some control over how information is collected and used. Data privacy is the capacity of an individual or group to prevent information about him or her from being known to anyone other than those to whom the information is provided. With the digital storage and transfer of personal data, the rapid development of communication technologies in the past decades has made privacy an urgent policy issue while also changing the traditional understanding of privacy (Jain et al. 2016, p. 3). Data privacy is about determining how individuals control information about themselves. The history of the modern information society is built on the struggle of the state and business corporations to control citizens and limit their ability to protect their freedoms (Mai, 2016, p. 195).

With the development of new communication technologies, digitalization has spread to all areas of daily life. With the spread of digitalization, digital communication has become increasingly important. Digitization has had both positive and negative benefits. Digital communication can be expressed as data flow over devices connected to the internet through applications. Digital communication has its own characteristics. It is possible to rank them as follows: recordability, searchability, repeatability, misformatin, disinformation, fast access to information. The fact that digital communication is interactive and there is no time and place limit allows the globalization of communication. This means the global use of digital media. In digital environments used by large segments of the world, users' information is recorded, stored, and can be processed and reused if desired. This process, which is often done without the consent of the individual, creates data security and privacy problems in digital environments.

With the increase in digital communication due to the fact that the Internet has become a necessity in daily life, the data has been recorded continuously and regularly. Individuals do their daily activities online. This situation causes a large amount of data to be shared in digital media. People consciously or unconsciously disclose their personal information while performing their daily activities. The user leaves digital traces about himself through activities such as grocery shopping, paying taxes, reading news, listening to music, reading books, shopping, and sharing photos. In addition, users share about their private lives. While Allen called it the "great privacy give away", Nissenbaum defined it as "media exhibitionism" (Allen, 2013, p. 847; Nissenbaum, 2010, p. 106).

Each user's digital footprints shape an individual's digital life. Personal information is collected, processed and reused with big data methods. Solove (2008), quoting from Murphy, defines personal information as "any data about an individual that identifies that individual". Tan and Pivot (2015) stated that personal information is information that can be used to identify a person. Personal information is defined as "information recorded in any form relating to an identifiable person". In the context of big data, privacy information is data that directly or indirectly includes personal information (Tan & Pivot, 2015, p. 861). Tan and Pivot (2015, p. 861) stated that personal information includes the following elements:

1- Race, national or ethnic origin, color, religion, age or marital status;
2- Education or medical, criminal or employment history, and financial transactions;
3- Any identifying number, symbol or other particular assigned to the individual, the address, fingerprints or blood type;
4- The personal opinions or views, the views or opinions of another individual about the individual;
5- The views or opinions of another individual about a proposal for a grant, an award or a prize to be made to the individual by an institution or a part of an institution;
6- The name of the individual where it appears with other personal information relating to the individual or where the disclosure of the name itself would reveal information about the individual
7- An individual who is or was performing services under contract for a government institution that relates to the services performed, including the terms of the contract, the name of the individual and the opinions or views of the individual given in the course of the performance of those services;
8- Any discretionary benefit of a financial nature, including the granting of a license or permit, conferred on an individual, including the name of the individual and the exact nature of the benefit.

While effective activities in the field of networking in the digital age offer many new opportunities, it can lead to risks for the protection of personal data. This poses certain challenges in terms of privacy in the digital space. The need for policies in this direction is increasing day by day. The main purpose is to ensure reliable protection of the individual in the digital age. Protecting users against online privacy and security, hacking and online threats has become imperative. Universal law defines privacy, personal data processing, protection of personal communication, processing of personal data for social media and other platforms as a fundamental human rights. With globalization, the traditional understanding of privacy has changed. The GDPR has introduced the right to be forgotten to regulate the processes in this area. The first paradigm interprets the right of everyone to choose the reason and way of processing information in their personal life. The second paradigm states the right of the individual owner of personal data to request deletion if not required (Romansky, 2022, p. 93).

Has Privacy Ended?

Data privacy and privacy have become issues that are frequently encountered in daily life in the information society. Neil Postman questioned the change that took place with the introduction of the computer into people's lives. Postman emphasizes that matters pertaining to the private lives of these people are easily accessible to those in power. People have become easier to track and control. People have begun to be perceived as objects expressed by numbers in the information society (Postman, 2006, p. 21).

Complaints about the end of privacy are at the center of current analysis of social media. In particular, the disclosure of information about state actors by Snowden brought the issue of systematic data collection and analysis to the fore. In the information society, information, personal data and communication are the new resources in the internet economy. This poses a risk to privacy. Postman (2006) in his book Technopoly: The New World Order mentions that there are people who believe that technical progress is humanity's greatest achievement. These people believe that technical progress will solve the biggest impasses. These people believed that information was a structure that would provide more freedom, creativity and vitality through the continuous and uncontrolled production and dissemination of information. Postman emphasizes that information does not accomplish any of these (Postman, 2006, p. 87). The continuous and uncontrolled production and dissemination of information has raised privacy issues due to data privacy.

Protection of personal data and privacy of everyone is a fundamental right. The right to privacy, freedom of expression, the right to personal security, the right to refuse self-incrimination, etc. creates a common basis for privacy is often associated with Westin's (1967) definition: "Privacy is the claim of individuals, groups, or institutions to determine when, how, and to what extent information about them is communicated to others." The right to privacy is the right to protect the space around us, which includes everything that is a part of us, such as body, home, property, thoughts, feelings, secrets and identity. The right to privacy allows us to choose the parts of this area that are accessible to others, and to manage the way and time of use (Romansky, 2022, p. 92). Burgoon (1982) evaluates privacy under four headings: "physical, interaction, psychological privacy and information privacy". Physical privacy is the absence of surveillance and control of one's physical space; interaction privacy "control over social encounters"; psychological privacy is "protection from intrusion into one's thoughts, feelings, attitudes, etc." and information confidentiality is about having control over the information that circulates and is stored about oneself.

Mai (2016) mentions two approaches to conceptualizing data privacy. These are restricted access and control theory. In restricted access, an individual can restrict others from receiving information about him or her. This understanding assumes that an individual will benefit from privacy by restricting access to their personal data. Control theory is associated with the restricted access tradition. Control theory is about an individual's ability to control who has access to information about an individual. The central element in the control tradition is the ability of individuals to control whether access to information about themselves is limited or unrestricted to others (Mai, 2016, p. 194). Solove (2002) argues privacy can be divided into six headings:

1. the right to be left alone;
2. limited access to the self, or the ability to shield oneself from unwanted others;
3. secrecy, or the concealment of certain matters from others;
4. control over personal information about oneself;
5. personhood, or the protection of one's personality, individuality and dignity; and
6. intimacy, which is to say control over, or limited access to, one's intimate relationships or aspects of life.

Solove (2013) argues that the dilemma of consent is at the core of many privacy issues. Privacy is based on the idea that people have the right or opportunity to give consent to provide requested personal data. Stating that the basic approach to privacy has not changed since the 1970s, Solove (2013) states that the consent approach to privacy is no longer meaningful in the information society. Individuals make autonomous choices about the processing of their personal data in the information society. In digital applications, people consent to give their personal information without much thought, without reading or fully understanding the consent form. In addition, consent forms are often quite long and written in legal language that few people understand.

CONCLUSION

With the inventions that took place in the 19th century, a deep belief was formed in the developments in science and technique. In this period, factors such as objectivity, efficiency and expertise, which ensure the success of inventions, gained great importance. However, individuals are no longer perceived as citizens, but as consumers. This situation has started to come to the fore with the development and spread of digital technologies. Individuals have become objects that must be consumed. The way of collecting the data of individuals who have become consumers with digital has changed. By following the digital traces left by individuals on digital platforms, content suitable for individuals has begun to be created with micro-targeting methods. Harold Innis talks about the monopoly of information in his book The Bias of Communication. Innis says that those who have control over the way a particular technology works have power over those who lack it. They inevitably form a set up against those who lack this power. In the digital age, technology holders hold users' data in their hands and shape the order.

Globalization is a fundamental feature of contemporary society with an increasing level of information. The development of information and communication technologies, which has a great impact on social and economic transformation, has caused many areas to move to the virtual environment, from business life to education. This situation, which increases productivity and efficiency economically, has created important problems in terms of the privacy of individuals. In the information age, individuals have become objects out of the subject position. It is possible to make some suggestions about protecting privacy for individuals whose privacy is violated by collecting their personal data. Individuals must first be literate in digital matters. In addition, individuals should pay attention to the following points in order to protect their personal data and privacy:

1. While browsing the web, it is necessary to be aware that the digital traces of individuals will endanger personal privacy.
2. You should not use a public, unauthenticated internet connection.
3. Private browsing should be used when searching, reading, watching a sensitive website or content.

4. User name and password should not be saved on any computer.
5. Always log out properly from password protected platforms.
6. Should not use public or free e-mail accounts for personal communication.
7. Confidential information should never be sent via e-mail and online telecommunications application.
8. Security settings of search engines should be enabled
9. Limited registration and use of social networks.
10. Attention should be paid to the security and privacy settings and disclaimers of social networks
11. Not to publish or share sensitive and confidential information on social networks
12. When not needed, the location tracking feature of the mobile phone should be turned off.
13. One should be aware of mobile applications on mobile devices.
14. Use the security and privacy settings and features in mobile phones and mobile applications.
15. It is always necessary to be aware that there is some kind of surveillance while working in public places.

In addition to these factors that users should pay attention to regarding personal data and privacy, supranational organizations and states should apply legal regulations and sanctions to protect personal data. The use of personal data should be regulated by a legal framework. It should be ensured that the parties using the data are transparent in this regard.

The information age requires a rethinking of the concept of privacy. In this age, how personal data is recorded and used has become a major concern. In the study, the privacy problem that arises as a result of recording and using personal data with the transfer of communication to this area with digitalization has been revealed. Violation of privacy allows capitalism to establish new forms of domination over the individual. With the increase in technical and socioeconomic transformations, the privacy problems that arise as a result of digital communication make it possible to criticize the increasing commodification of the social. In this context, it is hoped that this study will be expanded with studies on data security, privacy, data brokers and digital capitalism.

REFERENCES

Allen, A. L. (1988). *Uneasy access: Privacy for women in a free society*. Rowman & Littlefield.

Allen, A. L. 2013. An ethical duty to protect one's own information privacy? *Alabama Law Review* 64(4), 845–866.

Arslantaş-Toktaş, S., Binark, M., & Dikmen, E. S. (2012). Türkiye'de dijital gözetim [Digital surveillance in Turkey]. *Istanbul: Alternatif Bilişim Derneği*.

Bajpai, K., & Weber, K. (2017). Privacy in public: Translating the category of privacy to the digital age. In *From Categories to Categorization: Studies in Sociology, Organizations and Strategy at the Crossroads*. Emerald Publishing Limited.

Bell, D. (2018). The coming of post-industrial society. In *Social Stratification* (pp. 1066-1077). Routledge.

Bostancı, M. (2015). *Sosyal medya ve siyaset*. Palet Yayınları. Konya.

Burgoon, J. K. (1982). Privacy and communication. *Annals of the International Communication Association*, 6(1), 206-249.

Cullen, R., & Reilly, P. (2008). Information privacy and trust in government: A citizen-based perspective from New Zealand. *Journal of Information Technology & Politics*, 4(3), 61-80.

Freud, S. (1961). *Civilization and its discontents: College Ed*. Norton.

Jain, P., Gyanchandani, M., & Khare, N. (2016). Big data privacy: a technological perspective and review. *Journal of Big Data*, 3(1), 1-25.

Kara, N. (2021). Kamu kuruluşlarının iletişim ağlarının veri güvenliği: Mustafa Kemal Üniversitesi üzerine bir araştırma. Nil Çokluk (Ed.) In *Bilgi Çağında Siyaset Siyasal İletişim ve Büyük Veri* (p. 309-350). Ankara: Nobel Yayınları.

Mai, J. E. (2016). Big data privacy: The datafication of personal information. *The Information Society*, 32(3), 192-199.

McLuhan, M., & Powers, B. R. (1989). *The global village: Transformations in world life and media in the 21st century*. Communication and society.

Nissenbaum, H. (2010). *Privacy in context: Technology, policy, and the integrity of social life*. Stanford, CA: Stanford University Press.

Postman, N. (2006). *Teknopoli: Yeni dünya düzeni*. İstanbul, Paradigma.

Romansky, R. (2022). Digital age and personal data protection. *International Journal on Information Technologies & Security, 14*(3), 89-100.

Savaş, S. (2021). Siyasal iletişimde dijital izler. Nil Çokluk (Ed.) In Bilgi Çağında Siyaset Siyasal İletişim ve Büyük veri (p. 163-182). Ankara: Nobel Yayınları.

Seubert, S., & Becker, C. (2019). The culture industry revisited: Sociophilosophical reflections on 'privacy'in the digital age. Philosophy & Social Criticism, 45(8), 930-947.

Solove, D. J. (2002). Conceptualizing privacy. *Calif. L. Rev., 90,* 1087.

Solove, D. J. 2008. *Understanding privacy.* Cambridge, MA: Harvard University Press.

Solove, D. J. 2013. Privacy self-management and the consent dilemma. *Harvard Law Review* 126, 1880–1903.

Tan, Q., & Pivot, F. (2015). Big data privacy: changing perception of privacy. In *2015 IEEE International Conference on Smart City/SocialCom/Sustain-Com (SmartCity)* p. 860-865. IEEE.

Özcan, Z., & Savaş, S. (2021). Sanal topluluk platformu olarak Discord. *NOSYON: Uluslararası Toplum ve Kültür Çalışmaları Dergisi,* (7), 120-132.

Wessels, B. (2012). Identification and the practices of identity and privacy in everyday digital communication. *New media & society, 14*(8), 1251-1268.

Westin, A. F. (1967). *Privacy and freedom.* New York: Atheneum.

DATA SECURITY IN THE SCOPE OF BIG DATA MADNESS AND PRIVACY

*Nurat KARA**

INTRODUCTION

Individuals abundant in the industrial society's political, economic, social, and cultural areas have been positioned as individuals with the courtesies provided by communication technologies with the transition to the information society. In the new communication environment, expressed as mass-self communication (Castells, 2013, p. 20-21), individuals intentionally or unconsciously leave digital traces and continually generate data in their daily lives, which they maintain through technology. Realizing every moment of everyday life using information and communication technologies conveys the recording of the behaviors of citizens as consumers as data. These recorded data show a tremendous increase in quantitative and qualitative terms daily, and abstract and tangible values are produced from these processed data utilizing the software.

In addition, data; is available as structured, semi-structured, and unstructured. On the other hand, this data is produced in two ways: human and machine interactions. The characteristic feature of this situation, conceptualized as big data, is a continuous flow in data production. Although the density of the amount of data is essential, the primary significance fibs in transforming big data into value by analyzing it to manage. In addition to

* PhD, Head of IT Department, Hatay Mustafa Kemal University, nkara@mku.edu.tr

constructing retrospective analyzes with big data, forward-looking predictions are also made (Öcal, 2019). Computer scientists, physicists, economists, mathematicians, political scientists, bioinformaticians, sociologists, and other academics access the vast amount of information produced by and about people, objects, and their interactions. Numerous studies have been conducted on the potential benefits and costs of analyzing genetic sequences, social media interactions, health records, phone records, government records, and other digital traces left by people.

Important questions are whether big data will help us create good tools and services, or a wave of privacy breaches and invasive marketing; will it help us understand the online community and political movements, or will it be used to monitor and suppress protesters (Boyd & Crawford, 2012, p. 662).

Through big data technologies, billions of data per day occur, which requires analysis in various methods on the internet and mobile devices. Big data technologies have paved the way for incredible advances in many areas, from the public, astrophysics, health, social sciences, and commercial business practices to the fight against crime. However, using personal data in transactions made in the electronic environment violates the law and the rules of honesty. It has likewise increased the risk that they or their information may be disclosed and easily transferred to other places without the consent of the persons. This situation necessitates some regulations for the protection of personal data. It is essential for the confidentiality of personal data in the directives, traffic, and location.

Big Data and Its Social Effects

Big data is a large data set, typically from many diverse sources. It is one of the most valuable assets in today's digital world. The problem with big data is the security aspect- much sensitive and confidential information is out there, exposing businesses to potential privacy breaches. Companies are implementing considerable data security measures to keep their customers' information to address these concerns.

Big data can be overwhelming with a plethora of data available to us. We are not only faced with the challenge of sifting through it but also deciding what information is essential and needs to be protected. The security concerns that arise are not just about protecting personal data for individuals but large organizations vulnerable to hacking and government surveillance.

Big data, an important concept produced by the digitalizing world, has become a part of life in many areas, from social media to security systems, health, and finance. When the data is large, the value of the outputs to be produced is expected to be extensive (Chen, Chiang, & Storey, 2012). It is best to analyze the data according to its structure to deliver the expected value from big data. Big data is a concept that emerged to overcome the difficulties encountered in the management, analysis, storage, interpretation, and visualization of complex data that exceed the limits of traditional systems and cannot be processed in an acceptable time (Nandini & Pratheek, 2015; Victor, Abawajy, & Lopez, 2016). Components such as value, variability, vulnerability, and visualization have been added to the concept of big data, which has volume, velocity, diversity, and value components following the needs of problems that change over time (Victor, Abawajy, & Lopez, 2016; Tanwar & R. Duggal, 2015).

Traditional data security is network- and system-centric; however, today's multi-cloud architectures spread data across more platform-agnostic locations and incorporate more data types than ever. It must be an integral part of the cloud integration and data management strategy:

- The key to protecting the privacy of big data while still optimizing its value is an ongoing review of four critical data management activities.
- Privacy advocates are concerned about the threat to privacy represented by increasing storage and integration of

personally identifiable information; expert panels have released various policy recommendations to conform practice to expectations of privacy.

- The misuse of big data in several cases by media, companies, and even the government has allowed for the abolition of trust in every fundamental institution holding up society.

Big data privacy involves professionally managing big data to minimize risk and protect sensitive data. Because big data comprises large and complex data sets, many traditional privacy processes cannot oversee the scale and velocity required. To safeguard big data and ensure it can be used for analytics. It is essential to create a framework for privacy protection that can handle the volume, velocity, variety, and value (Oweis, Owais, George, Suliman, & Snášel, 2015) of big data is moved between environments, processed, analyzed, and shared.

There are many privacy concerns and government regulations for big data platforms. In an era of multi-cloud computing, data owners must keep up with the pace of data growth and the proliferation of regulations that govern it especially regulations protecting the privacy of sensitive data and personally identifiable information (PII) (Bernstein, 2021). With more data spread across more locations, the business risk of a privacy breach has never been higher, and with it, consequences range from high fines to loss of market share.

In big data analytics, Hadoop and Spark are the most used mainframe technologies in the literature. Hadoop processes the data it keeps in the Hadoop File System (HDFS) per the MapReduce structure; Spark, on the other hand, allows the data it maintains in temporary memory as a Resilient Distributed Dataset (RDD) to be processed with an adapted version of the MapReduce structure. Which technology is preferred depends on the problem? For example; If an analytics application will be made on streaming data, using Spark is more advantageous than Hadoop, while Hadoop can be more advantageous than Spark in processing data that is on the disk (Samadi, Zbakh, & Tadonki, 2016; Lee, Kim, Nam, & Shin, 2017).

Big data security is an umbrella term that includes all security measures and tools applied to analytics and data processes. Attacks on big data systems – information theft, DDoS attacks, ransomware, or other malicious activities – can originate offline or online and crash a system.

The advent of Big Data has important implications for privacy and will result in increased risks of privacy breaches. The benefits of Big Data are myriad, but the danger is that people could be subject to profiling, and decisions could be made without the individuals knowing the reasons for such findings. Privacy audits may be a method of addressing these concerns. To guard against the possibility of a loss of autonomy and individual liberty, "big data will require monitoring and transparency, which will require new types of expertise and institutions." For example, some tertiary institutions in the United States that have sufficient resources are using the social media history of individual applicants as a screening process, assisting in determining whether to admit a student to college. The potential students are sometimes not informed that their information has been used this way. Privacy concerns of consumers are significant. In research by the Federal Trade Commission ('FTC'), a nationwide survey indicated that 57 percent of all app users have either uninstalled an app over concerns about sharing their personal information or declined to install an app in the first place for similar reasons (Madden & Smith, 2012).

Big data privacy is also a matter of customer trust. The more data is collected about users, the easier it gets to "connect the dots" to understand their current behavior, draw inferences about their future behavior, and develop deep and detailed profiles of their lives and preferences. It is to be transparent with the customers about what is being done with their data, how it is storing it, and what steps should be taken to comply with privacy and data protection regulations.

As part of their overall big data security management strategy, companies with solid data governance policies are better prepared to cope with attacks that penetrate multiple ports of entry and compromise the integrity of data used for analytics, strategic planning, and operational decision-making. Nevertheless, governance policies are not enough. Vendors and service providers acclimate to the scope of cyberattacks, GDPR and California Consumer Privacy Act (CCPA) regulations, and traditional data management tools and services are being contorted and extended (Karjian, 2021). They are also being increasingly injected with AI and machine learning capabilities to keep pace with the increased number of petabyte-sized applications, particularly in the cloud.

Data managers are forever vigilant when protecting the integrity and privacy of their precious data stores. The security and privacy challenges sparked by an onslaught of data breaches and malware attacks over the past few years and the new wave of consumer privacy regulations have been exacerbated by the effects of the COVID-19 pandemic, which accelerated the transition of the digital workforce to a remote work environment.

How is Privacy Possible in Big Data Madness?

Privacy is a multifaceted variable concept that can vary from society to society, culture to culture, and even individual to individual. Privacy-Preserving Data Publishing (PPDP) models; are the structures that cover the data privacy protection process and the parties in this process, which ensure that the data is published while preserving privacy to generate more value from the data. Data that cannot be managed with traditional architecture and systems in terms of volume, speed, and diversity is considered big data, thus bringing new requirements. For the field of data privacy, where cyber threats have recently intensified, the solutions to be developed in the area of big data must be explicitly designed for the needs of this field. Publishing while protecting the privacy of big data is significant in producing outputs that will benefit the country, such as analysis, research, providing added value, making plans, and creating policies.

Since big data systems are high-cost structures, installing such systems in a single central facility is more cost-effective than separately under different roofs.

Data Privacy is a big challenge in this digital world. It aims to safeguard personal or sensitive information from cyberattacks, breaches, and intentional or unintentional data loss. Businesses must follow stricter Data Privacy principles with the help of access management services in the cloud, including very rigid privacy compliance, to strengthen Data Protection. It is best to follow a few rules alongside implementing one or more Data Security technologies. The general rules are knowing the data, having more grip over the data stores and backup, safeguarding the network against unauthorized access, conducting regular risk assessments, and training the users regularly about Data Privacy and Data Security.

Data privacy is defined in the literature as "selective informational control" (Chibba & Cavoukian, 2015) and "the correct use of the information of the addressee and the decision mechanism to share which information of the addressee with whom and to what extent" (Jain, Gyanchandani, & Khare, 2016). In addition to these definitions, the presented below will help understand the subject better:

- Minimizing the risk of disclosure of data owners as much as possible with any method, technical or background information to be applied to the data,
- To prevent, as much as possible, direct or indirect access to one or more persons from the data,
- Selective control of the data subject in determining the limits on who, at what level, and for what purpose the data will be shared, and
- It is the elimination, as far as possible, of any relationship that will enable access from the data to the person.

Big data is a term that refers to the collection and analysis of data sets so large and complex that it becomes difficult to process using traditional computer systems. Data security is crucial for many organizations, especially companies with sensitive data. Recently, we have seen an increase in cyberattacks against businesses and government agencies. The damage caused ranges from leaked customer data to stolen intellectual property.

Data security and cyber security are essential for any organization, regardless of size. No one can access the data that companies have collected over the years. It is where data security software comes in; whether on-premises or a cloud-based solution, it helps protect customer data from theft or accidental disclosure.

Cyber security is a critical component of any company, and many cybersecurity solutions are available to businesses. However, some solutions can be too expensive for small companies or lack the necessary features for large organizations. The best cybersecurity solution will depend on their business size and needs.

A brief introduction to Big Data, the importance of Security and Privacy in Big Data, and the challenges required to overcome applying Machine Learning techniques to Big Data are provided. Expand Big data privacy involves effectively managing big data to minimize risk and protect sensitive data. Because big data comprises large and complex data sets, many traditional privacy processes cannot control the scale and velocity required. To safeguard big data and ensure it can be used for analytics, the need to create a framework for privacy protection that can oversee the volume, velocity, variety, and value of big data as it is moved between environments, processed, analyzed, and shared.

There are many privacy concerns and government regulations for big data platforms. However, knowing what is happening with the data and where the data is stored is essential for organizations and private users. The key to protecting the privacy of the big data while still optimizing its value is an ongoing review of four critical data management activities:

Based on the enlisted concerns, it is apparent why enterprises are seeing Big Data Security as a significant concern. However, the good news is that many such challenges can be quickly addressed with the correct information, resources, skilled workforce, detailed coping strategy, and commitment to data integrity and privacy. The absence of threats to Big Data will lead businesses to achieve their goal of harnessing data for better customer experience and enhanced customer retention.

How will the data security scale keep up with data breaches and insider threats as they become common? In an era of multi-cloud computing, data owners must keep up with the pace of data growth and the proliferation of regulations that govern it. With more data spread across more locations, the business risk of a privacy breach has never been higher, and with it, consequences range from high fines to loss of market share.

The volume and velocity of data from existing sources, such as legacy applications and e-commerce, are expanding fast. They also have new (and growing) varieties of data types and seeds, such as social networks and IoT device streams. Keeping pace, the big data privacy strategy must also expand. That requires them to consider all these issues:

The work investigates the various properties that characterize big data, problems, issues related to extensive handling, and a broad view of the security and privacy issues related to big data analysis. The work ends with a glimpse into the future trends the world of big data will see.

Today, Big Data is crucial for any business to succeed in the data-driven world. With several advanced infrastructures, organizations have streamlined data flow for real-time insights delivery and better decision-making. However, Big Data brings several security risks that could negatively impact organizations. Incorporating security measures while storing and processing Big Data can lead to data breaches. While simplifying the accessibility of data is essential for companies, having control over Big Data is equally crucial for ensuring trust among its customers.

Many companies use big data analytics tools to improve business strategies. That gives cyber criminals more opportunities to attack significant data architecture. Thus, the list of big data security issues continues to grow. Data mining is the heart of many big data environments. Data mining tools find patterns in unstructured data. The problem is that data often contains personal and financial information. Therefore, companies must add extra security layers to protect against external and internal threats.

The consequences of information theft can be even worse when organizations store sensitive or confidential information like credit card numbers or customer information. They may face fines because they failed to meet basic data security measures to comply with data loss protection and privacy mandates like the General Data Protection Regulation (GDPR).

Data Security Process in Big Data Technologies

If we can no longer escape to the safety of our home to escape commercialization, and if we cannot run to our house, there is no escape (Ritzer, 2000). Anthony Giddens states that "privacy has transformed" with neo-liberalism and says that as an integral part of the reflexivity of modernity, the self is structured as a reflexive project, and the individual has to find his own identity among the strategies and options provided by abstract systems (Giddens, 1994). In other words, all our private spaces, the establishment of our privacy, our intimate relationships, our moments, our moments, and our stories are far from an ideal state that is free from the strong influence of neo-liberal globalization, independent of external factors, shaped only by our desires and decisions, and whose rules we set. Intimacies are only shaped through their direct and symbolic interventions within neo-liberal global feelings, desires, ideas, and expressions (Özbay, 2011).

Artificial intelligence, also known as AI, is a machine's simulation of human intelligence. Machine learning is a subset of AI that enables computers to learn from data and make predictions based on previous events. An often-debated topic about the future of AI is its ability to cause more harm than good in society. Many experts believe that AI will lead to advancements in healthcare and education because it will

The amount of data collected and stored has increased exponentially over the last few years. This data is gathered in many ways, including search terms, social media posts, location, and consumption habits. However, with all this data being collected comes the issue of security and safety. What happens if hackers can access this information? What will happen if this information falls into the wrong hands?

Data security is one of the most pressing issues of the future. With the rise of big data technologies, it has become necessary to ensure that our information is secure and private. It can be achieved through various methods, including encryption and access controls.

CONCLUSION

Rapid developments in information and communication technologies, especially after the globalization wave seen in the 1980s, have irreversibly changed the life process of human beings. All information and communication technologies, which are actively involved in all areas of life that modern people need to maintain their life and provide stability, have become a part of people without awareness.

Rapid developments in information and communication technologies, especially after the globalization wave seen in the 1980s, have irreversibly changed the life process of human beings. All information and communication technologies, which are actively involved in all areas of life that modern people need to maintain their life and provide stability, have become a part of people without awareness. As a result of these developments over time, McLuhan's "Technology is the Extension of Human" theory, in which he said, "Technologies are not just inventions people use, they are tools that reinvent people." has become a reality (Altay, 2003). While technology has become one of the necessities of daily life for today's people, it has become a part of the individual without realizing it. People have been restructured with technology. Although individuals lead a life so intertwined with technology, it is a situation that makes their lives easier and liberates the individual; at the same time, it restricts the individual's freedom and undermines the increasingly important concept of privacy. Hal Niedzviecki, in his book "Peep Culture," explains how digital technology, communication tools, and social networking networks cover our lives today and mirror today's society with examples. Niedzviecki, who claims that information is collected from people through the internet and social media and that this data inspires companies for innovative marketing tactics, conveys the cyclicity experienced with the following words: "Many of us do not perceive these practices as detention or do not think that our private lives have been interfered with. We see discounts and campaigns as rewarding our loyalty to the company. We show loyalty to this company, chain stores or international company and in return, we get a discount" (Uçkan, 2010). We do not care what the company does with the information we provide. Besides, they do not like to talk much about this subject and do not collect information directly. However, they may sell the information we voluntarily give them to other companies, research companies, and even the government. Thus, our file is filled with details they cannot learn through legal means. For example, these files may be sold to other databases, banks, and companies doing market research (Uçkan, 2010).

Today, social media sites are among the most valuable structures of the internet with the highest commercial potential. Therefore, social media sites are commercial establishments; although they are very natural, their content is "they" created by their users. The fact that they see their members as customers and can "sell" their information and photos to different institutions raises the question of respect for the privacy of sites such as Facebook, YouTube, and Twitter. From the moment of access to the internet, all searches made, e-mails sent, pages viewed, photos liked, messages written, and retweets made are recorded and marketed over an exchange value "when the day comes." Facebook founder Mark Zuckerberg's words that "privacy is out of date" and Google CEO Eric Schmidt's statement that "if you have something to hide, do not share it" clearly show companies' views of privacy (Uçkan, 2010). Surveillance changes form and become more manageable through new communication technologies. Surrounded by these technologies, individuals are forced to choose between security and freedom; These tools, which offer the promise of liberty to individuals, also restrict privacy. Individuals in digital society face new, different, and more complex dangers than before (Çalık & Toker, 2016, p. 9).

Privacy and big data are in constant conflict with each other. Collecting personal information for marketing is a significant issue, especially on social media sites like Facebook. These sites contain a lot of personal data that can be used to identify individuals' tastes and preferences.

Data security, privacy, and big data are at the forefront of today's concerns. As more data is collected and stored by companies, there is a greater need to ensure that the information is secure.

Privacy advocates are concerned about the threat to privacy represented by increasing storage and integration of personally identifiable information; expert panels have released various policy recommendations to conform practice to expectations of privacy. The misuse of big data in several cases by media, companies, and even the government has allowed for the abolition of trust in every fundamental institution holding up society.

This handbook examines the effect of cyberattacks, data privacy laws, and COVID-19 on evolving big data security management tools and techniques:

Data managers step up measures to protect the integrity of their data while complying with GDPR and CCPA regulations.

Companies turn to exist data governance and security best practices in the wake of the pandemic.

We look at the importance of corporate culture, communication, and education in determining the success of data governance and its parent, data management.

Big data has been used in policing and surveillance by institutions like law enforcement and corporations. Due to the less visible nature of data-based administration as compared to traditional methods of policing, objections to big data policing are less likely to arise.

Nayef Al-Rodhan argues that a new social contract will be needed to protect individual liberties in the context of big data and giant corporations that own vast amounts of information and that big data should be monitored and better regulated at the national and international levels. Barocas and Nissenbaum argue that one way of protecting individual users is by being informed about the types of information being collected, with whom it is shared, under what constraints, and for what purposes.

Encrypted search and cluster formation in big data was demonstrated in March 2014 at the American Society of Engineering Education. Gautam Siwach, engaged in Tackling the challenges of Big Data by MIT Computer Science and Artificial Intelligence Laboratory and Amir Esmailpour at the UNH Research Group, investigated the key features of big data as the formation of clusters and their interconnections. They focused on the security of big data and the orientation of the term towards the presence of diverse types of data in an encrypted form at a cloud interface by providing the basic definitions and real time examples within the technology. Moreover, they proposed an approach for identifying the encoding technique to advance toward an expedited search over encrypted text leading to security enhancements in big data.

The evolution of technology has given rise to new techniques to share, process, and store data. These innovative technologies have often been introduced without a prior assessment of the impact on privacy and data protection, while new threats and attack vectors have introduced additional challenges. The use and adoption of big data within governmental processes allow cost, productivity, and innovation efficiencies but do not come without flaws. Data analysis often requires multiple parts of government (central and local) to collaborate and create new and innovative processes to deliver the desired outcome. A typical government organization that uses big data is the National Security Administration (NSA), which constantly monitors the internet's activities in search of potential patterns of suspicious or illegal activities their system may pick up.

The General Data Protection Regulation (GDPR) addresses the risks associated with personal processing data. The regulation intends to reinforce individuals' rights in the digital era and enable them to control their data better online. At the same time, modernized and unified rules will allow businesses to make the most of the Digital Single Market (DSM) opportunities, benefiting from increased consumer trust.

If these potential problems are not corrected or regulated, the effects of big data policing may continue to shape societal hierarchies. The conscientious usage of big data policing could prevent individual-level biases from becoming institutional biases, Brayne also notes. Especially since 2015, big data has become prominent in business operations as a tool to help employees work more efficiently and streamline information technology (IT) collection and distribution. The use of big data to resolve IT and data collection issues within an enterprise is called IT operations analytics (ITOA). By applying significant data principles to machine intelligence and deep computing concepts, IT departments can predict potential issues and prevent them. ITOA businesses offer platforms for systems management that bring data silos together and generate insights from the whole of the system rather than from isolated pockets of data.

To this end, ENISA investigates the solutions offered by privacy by design as a fundamental principle of embedding data protection safeguards at the heart of new electronic products and services. An example is Privacy Enhancing Technologies (PETs), which can support privacy integration in systems and services. ENISA also analyses other security measures concerning cryptographic protocols or online and mobile data protection, among others.

On Data Protection Day, the European Union Agency for Cybersecurity (ENISA) explores how to engineer data protection principles. Portability and interconnectivity are socio-technical features of big data. A 2018 definition states, "Big data is where parallel computing tools are needed to oversee data," and notes, "This represents a distinct and clearly defined change in the computer science used, via parallel programming theories, and losses of some of the guarantees and capabilities made by Codd's relational model."

REFERENCES

Altay, D. (2003). Küresel köyün medyatik mimarı: Marshall McLuhan. In G. B. Nurdogan Rigel, *Kadife Karanlık* (pp. 1-73). İstanbul: Su Publications.

Bernstein, C. (2021). *Personally identifiable information (PII)*. Retrieved from techtarget.com: https://www.techtarget.com/searchsecurity/definition/personally-identifiable-information-PII#:~:text=Personally%20identifiable%20information%20(PII)%20is,anonymous%20data%20is%20considered%20PII.

Boyd, D., & Crawford, K. (2012). Critical questions for big data. Information. *Communication & Society, 15*(5), 662-679.

Castells, M. (2013). *Communication power*. Oxford: Oxford University Press.

Chen, H., Chiang, R. H., & Storey, V. (2012). Business intelligence and analytics: From big data to big impact. *MIS, 36*(4).

Chibba, M., & Cavoukian, A. (2015). Privacy, consumer trust and big data: Privacy by design and the 3 C'S. *IEEE ITU Kaleidoscope: Trust in the Information Society.*

Çalık, D., & Toker, G. (2016). Ekran çağı insanı ve dijital toplum. *XXI. Yüzyılda Türkiye'de İnternet Konferansı*. 3-5 Kasım 2016 Ankara: : TED Üniversitesi.

Giddens, A. (1994). *Mahremiyetin dönüşümü – modern toplumlarda cinsellik, aşk ve erotizm*. İstanbul: Ayrıntı Yayınları.

Jain, P., Gyanchandani, M., & Khare, N. (2016). Big data privacy: a technological perspective and review. *Journal of Big Data, 3*(1), 25.

Karjian, R. (2021). *Big data security management embraces governance, privacy.* Retrieved from techtarget.com: https://www.techtarget.com/searchdata-management/ehandbook/Big-data-security-management-embraces-governance-privacy

Lee, M.-S., Kim, E., Nam, C.-S., & Shin, D.-R. (2017). Design of educational big data application using spark. *IEEE International Conference on Advanced Communication Technology.* Bongpyeong, South Korea.

Madden, M., & Smith, A. (2012, September 5). *Privacy and data management on mobile devices.* Retrieved from pewresearch.org: https://www.pewresearch.org/internet/2012/09/05/privacy-and-data-management-on-mobile-devices-2/

Nandini, K. S., & Pratheek, T. (2015). Providing anonymity using top down specialization on big data using hadoop framework. *IEEE India Conference.* India.

Oweis, N. E., Owais, S. S., George, W., Suliman, M. G., & Snášel, V. (2015). *A survey on big data, mining: (Tools, Techniques, Applications and Notable Uses) intelligent data analysis and applications.* New York Dordrecht London: Springer Cham Heidelberg.

Öcal, D. (2019). Teknolojik yeniliklerin yönetimi ve tüketen bireyin dönüşümü. *Karadeniz İletişim Araştırmaları Dergisi,* 97-115.

Özbay, C. (2011). *Giriş: Neoliberalizm ve mahremiyet.* İstanbul: Metis yayınları.

Ritzer, G. (2000). *Büyüsü bozulmuş dünyayı büyülemek.* (Ş. S. Kaya, Trans.) İstanbul: Ayrıntı yayınları.

Samadi, Y., Zbakh, M., & Tadonki, C. (2016). Comparative study between Hadoop and Spark based on Hibench benchmarks. *International Conference on Cloud Computing Technologies and Applications.* Marrakech, Morocco.

Tanwar, M., & R. Duggal, S. K. (2015). Unravelling unstructured data: A wealth of information in big data. in Reliability. *IEEE International Conference on Infocom Technologies and Optimization.* Noida, India.

Uçkan, Ö. (2010). *Mahremiyet ve sosyal medya.* Retrieved from bthaber.com.tr: http://bthaber.com.tr/?p>4806

Victor, N., Abawajy, J. H., & Lopez, D. (2016). Privacy models for big data: a survey. *International Journal of Big Data Intelligence, 3*(1), 61-75.

DIGITAL LITERACY IN INCREASING DATA SECURITY: AN EVALUATION FROM THE COMMUNICATOR'S PERSPECTIVE

*Mehmet KARANFİLOĞLU**

INTRODUCTION

Many communication means persistence in changing both individual and corporate lives. From the communication perspective, utilizing these tools is vital regarding the tools' diversity and users. However, this diversification in information communication technologies likewise creates tremendous data production. These data, produced in massive quantities, are circulated in the internet universe uncontrollably, driving info and data security-sensitive. When considered from a communicative point of view, digital literacy emerges from applying basic security steps for the privacy and protection of this data digital literacy guides in using these media tools and shows how to use these tools more safely. Therefore, accurate reading and proper use of digital media tools emerge as essential elements in data security, communication process continuity, and cybercrime prevention. This chapter aims to reveal these concepts, relations, and concerns about how communicative activities shall be overseen by assembling securer data usage from the digital literacy perspective.

Although the digitalization process has become noticeable in the last few years, a process in the 1960s shall be mentioned; in

---

* Assist. Prof., Ibn Haldun University, Communication Faculty New Media and Communication Department, mehmet.karanfiloglu@ihu.edu.tr

this process, many philosophers and theorists have focused on this issue and discussed some consequences. The world has become globally interconnected; Dijk claims developing countries have converted to a network society with the rapid spread of satellite television, mobile phones, and the internet and defines the 21st century as the "age of networks" (Dijk, 2016, p. 13).

The time when increasing data production with technology is widespread is named the post-industrial information society (Daniel Bell), information society (Alvin Toffler), global village (Marshall McLuhan), and some technologies produce and rapidly disseminate information as advanced technology. Castells points to this structure in conceptualizing the post-industrial information and network society. As the most effective means of transmission, the internet is the system that establishes a link between the network society and the information society. Transitioning from the industrial society to the information age, Castells states that new communication technologies accelerate globalization with fast and simultaneous communication by eliminating space. According to Castells, power relations are the basis of society in which power is used through networks. Accordingly, he discusses four different forms of power under social and technological conditions (Castells, 2011, p. 773):

1. Networking Power

2. Network Power

3. Networked Power

4. Network-making Power

For its part, the ability to understand, interpret and reproduce incoming information is related to literacy. While the process of understanding information brings the concept of literacy to the agenda, it is evident that many types of literacy gain paramountcy today; however, digital literacy is at the forefront of digital transformation and its benefits. The concept of *digital literacy* explains the competence of using tools so that the individual may search for and find accurate, reliable, scientific information sources.

Furthermore, individuals may analyze and synthesize the acquired information and their ability to think critically through network devices such as smartphones, tablets, laptops, and desktop computers. It includes finding, understanding, analyzing, producing, and sharing information. Technology and the new communication tools very popular in today's society are the actors of a parallel world living with humanity (Artut, 2014, p. 12).

It is not possible to discuss a single type of literacy today; the concept of literacy is increasingly referred to as digital literacy, media literacy, technology literacy, health literacy, internet literacy, risk literacy, computer literacy, environmental literacy, economic literacy, legal literacy, cultural literacy, intercultural literacy, political literacy. In addition, many other types of literacy have been popularized recently, such as consumer literacy, critical literacy, moral literacy, civic literacy, and web literacy (Kurbanoğlu, 2010, p. 739).

This study discusses digital literacy and other related literacy types as well as privacy and data security from a communication perspective.

The Future of Communication and Digital Literacy

As technology develops, the subject of communication becomes increasingly central; by digitalization, the consequence of communication has become more comprehensible than ever afore. Notwithstanding, some skills have lustered as humanity recenter; due to the rapid change and technological transformation, the skills that individuals need to acquire have undergone a significant difference compared to the last century (Ala-Mutka, 2011; Dede, 2010). These skills are believed to contain much information about what may happen in the future in communication; along with the changing skills, there has been a shift in the perception of traditional literacy defined in the middle of the 20th century, and alternative and contemporary literacy concepts have been replaced (Condy, Chigona, Gachago, & Ivala, 2012).

Literacy status indicates how many individuals have these skills, and having sufficient knowledge in terms of literacy brings along the ability to use communication technologies effectively and strategically. Previously, the definition of the traditional literacy concept and the primary purpose of non-formal education systems was to equip students with reading and writing skills in their mother tongue; this purpose began to be questioned in the middle of the 20th century (Kurt, Orhan, Yaman, Solak, & Türkan, 2014). When it comes to literacy, much more complex processes are on the list, conversely, many types of it are noted to define literacy more accurately.

With the emergence of digitalization since the 1960s, many concepts have emerged, such as computer literacy, *digital literacy*, information literacy, technology literacy, and information and communication technologies literacy, which are based on various cognitive, affective, and psychomotor competencies, especially technology and literacy skills (Leaning, 2019). In the 2010s, we encounter the concept of digital literacy with the increasing level of technological maturity and the effect of digital transformation along with other global factors. Eshet-Alkalai (2004) provides a conceptual framework that defines digital literacy as a compilation of five diverse types of literacy: photo-visual, reproductive, information, branched, and socio-emotional literacy. Nonetheless, when digital literacy is mentioned, some other concepts should be known; computer literacy, technology literacy, and media literacy. These three definitions of literacy are related to each other by reason of the fact that is knowing all three shall be considered as completing a part of a triple trivet. According to Oliver and Towers (2000), computer literacy has long been expressed as people's predisposition to their ability to use computers and information technologies by the definition of media literacy made by Aufderheide (1993). Accordingly, *media literacy* is defined as an individual's ability to decipher printed and electronic media tools, evaluate the data there, analyze these data, and produce data suitable for these media organs. Technology literacy, in other respects, has been a catalyst that includes human cognitive and psychomotor skills for the last ten years (Crowe, 2006). According to another definition, it is a way of thinking about how technology may become a tool to solve any problem (Herman, Maknun, Barliana, & Mardiana, 2019). Technology literacy is used, managed, evaluated, and understood by technology (ITEEA, 2000).

With the use of digital language in all communication technologies, there are three essential features of new media technologies that enroll personal lives: interaction, demassification, and asynchrony (Rogers, 2003). From this point of view, it is possible to make some predictions about digital literacy; however, there are many uncertainties in the definition of digital literacy (Eshet-Alkalai, 2004; Bawden, 2008). Forasmuch as the question of what digital components are may differentiate the meanings. Experts (Eshet-Alkalai & Amichai-Hamburger, 2004; Bawden, 2008) recommend many digital literacy components (Perdana, Yani, Jumadi, & Rosana, 2019). In this context, it is possible to consider digital literacy from various aspects.

Alkalai and Hamburger (2004) define digital literacy as photo-visual, reproduction, branching, information, and socio-emotional skills. Honan (2008) states that these skills; that breaking the code of texts is defined as participating in the meaning of the texts using the texts functionally, critically analyzing, and transforming the texts. Hague and Payton (2010, p. 19) define digital literacy more comprehensively with eight skill areas: functional skills, creativity, critical thinking and evaluation, cultural and social understanding, collaboration, finding and selecting information, effective communication, and e-safety. Hobbs, on the other side, approaches the subject from another angle. Hobbs (2010, p. 7) mentions that digital and media literacy must be combined, and education must be given in schools. Based on this, individuals who have media and digital literacy skills; are people who may access and share information through research, evaluate and analyze the quality and safety of digital content, as well as could create content, and apply ethical principles by acting socially (Hobbs, 2010, p. 7). According to Hobbs (2010, p. 7), digital literates are people who may take social action. Finally, Belshaw (2011, p. 206) tried determining the dimensions of digital literacy skills in his thesis study. Evaluating this skill in eight assorted sizes. Belshaw's classification deals with the elements of the craft rather than the characteristics of the digital literate individual:

1. Cultural
2. Cognitive
3. Constructive
4. Communicative
5. Confident
6. Creative
7. Critical
8. Civic

JISC (Joint Information Systems Committee), which likewise works on cyber-security, defines *digital literacy* as individuals who have the skills to live with digital technology, learn and work in this environment. Accordingly, digital literacy encompasses all the previously mentioned technology-based literacy. Therefore, the framework for digital literacy is explained through this definition (JISC, 2014):

- Media Literacy
- Communications and Collaboration
- Career and Identity Management
- ICT (Information Communication Technologies) Literacy
- Learning Skills
- Digital Scholarship
- Information Literacy

Data/ Information Privacy

Developments in communication and technologies dismay the world about security. The fact that individuals are more present on the internet and digital platforms has led to an enormous increase in digital data. Using this data brings many conveniences for both users and companies; however, it triggers many sensitive situations regarding data security. Data security requires careful use within the framework of some ethical principles during the collection, storage, and processing of the obtained data. Nevertheless, it is possible to deal with the issue within the framework of more than one dimension regarding data security. In this sense, there are dimensions of security, such as database security, communication network security, communication systems security, and access security, within the scope of ensuring personal data security (Şimşek, 2008, p. 85).

Databases are data sets that consist of the traces that individuals leave behind while browsing the Internet. Thanks to these sets, it becomes feasible to produce meaningful information. Without databases, companies cannot perform tasks such as estimation and measurement; however, this information may be sensitive information that may be considered personal and protected by law. Therefore, the security of databases is regarded as the first dimension. In the second and third stages, there are communication networks and systems where this data is obtained and used. Their safety is considered at least as important as primary care.

Consequently, deciding which data is sensitive at this stage is necessary. In this context, it is possible to divide the data into sensitive and non-sensitive data (Küzeci, 2010). Different persons may obtain sensitive data, and due to the nature of such data, it may cause the related persons to be victimized, offended, and discriminated against in different situations (Gündüz, 2022, p. 32). It is possible to call the remaining data as non-sensitive data.

Data security requires the protection of both types of information. Various platforms and institutions have set specific standards and principles to ensure data security. There are personal data security regulations at the international level, such as the United Nations, the European Court of Human Rights, the

Council of Europe, the Organization for Economic Co-operation and Development (OECD), the Universal Declaration of Human Rights (UDHR), and the European Union. Apart from international regulations, there are some accepted principles in data security. According to Gündüz, those may be listed as follows (2022, p. 30):

1. Critical and sensitive data should be prevented from being obtained unintentionally by unauthorized persons, and a guarantee of accessibility should be ensured only by those authorized to access it (Confidentiality).
2. Modification and deletion of data by persons other than the owner or authorized person should be prevented (Integrity).
3. The data or the systems in which the data is processed must be ready to be used continuously and work uninterruptedly (Availability).
4. The data owner's or authorized person's identity requires authentication (Authentication).

As can be seen, the issue of data security is susceptible and is given importance by many international institutions and organizations. In Turkey, the security of personal data is fundamental at the national level, and limits have been determined within the scope of the Personal Data Protection Law (known as KVKK *in Turkish*). However, although data security is considered essential by by-laws, conventions, and international institutions, the perception of privacy in data security is getting more sensitive daily.

The penetration of technology into all areas of life with intelligent devices, and the new media opportunities such as social media affecting increased users, raise the issues of surveillance and privacy. Sharing has become more widespread, bringing social media to the fore. Risks related to data and privacy security on social media platforms are always possible.

Although it may seem harmless and leisurely for users, social media has a high history of privacy and data security issues. Despite these benefits, the concerns and discussions about security and privacy issues in the social media environment never fall from the agenda (Patel, 2017, p. 836). For instance, on Facebook, in June 2013, due to an error, the e-mail addresses and phone numbers of approximately six million members were accessed without being requested (Newcomb, 2018). Another example, most notably, is the "Cambridge Analytica (data) scandal." It is the event that the personally identifiable information of millions of Facebook users (approximately fifty million) is collected by Cambridge Analytica, and the data obtained is used to influence the opinion of the voters on behalf of some politicians. Brittnay, former director of Cambridge Analytica after Wiley Kaiser, used expressions that people may change their minds with their method. After the data of the people called "persuasive" while targeting, this data allows them to vote by bombarding them with blogs, articles, and videos to change their behavior (Noujaim & Amer, 2019).

When it comes to social media, individuals need to be more careful when using these platforms. Because of new media opportunities, especially in social media, individuals may encounter difficulties such as inappropriate content, internet addiction, adverse effects, virtual fraud, identity theft, harassment, and cyberbullying (Altun, et al., 2018, p. 41-43). Hence, during the profile creation process on social networking sites, name, home address, e-mail address, and other confidential information are requested. Because of this information, there is no need to doubt that unknown and unwanted malicious persons may present various dangers (Chewae, Hayikader, Hasan, & Ibrahim, 2015, p. 1). If personal information is not used judiciously and reliably on social media, the user's privacy may be attacked in numerous ways. Because the social media environment is closely monitored, information, documents, and images should be shared as little as possible. All of this is constantly being archived and accumulated in the centers of social networks in the USA. The possibility that large images are created to be used for different purposes should never be underestimated (Ceylan, Demiryürek, &

Kandemir, 2015, p. 8). So even a single photo or video may result in an enemy accessing this information (Ghazinour & Ponchak, 2017, p. 267-268).

Regarding data security, social media results are not only encountered. In addition to this, especially in big data and data mining, the issue of data security is discussed, and the methods of ensuring privacy are mentioned. Data mining applications and mathematical analyzes should be made by considering personal privacy (Eyüpoğlu, Aydın, Sertbaş, Zaim, & Öneş, 2017). Regarding confidentiality, taking security measures between the computer layers may be necessary, as violations cause legal responsibilities and ethical problems. For instance, virtual barriers such as firewalls, secure socket layers, and transport layer security are designed to limit access to data (Eyüpoğlu, Aydın, Sertbaş, Zaim, & Öneş, 2017). To the contrary, it is tried to take measures for privacy by employing some additional elements. Organizations use a variety of de-identification methods (Eyüpoğlu, Aydın, Sertbaş, Zaim, & Öneş, 2017, p. 177) to ensure security and privacy.

Although such measures are sometimes aimed at ensuring privacy to a certain extent, they may likewise complicate the use of data. This situation may pose problems that hinder the development of some technologies. Therefore, the development of some technologies may be slower before security problems are overcome. Alternatively, a developing technology may be subjected to tests and procedures to overcome security barriers for a while. Passwords supervised access and two-factor authentication; are technical solutions nonetheless low-level that are extensively used to ensure security and privacy when data is shared and aggregated in dynamic and distributed data systems. The more advanced technical solution is cryptography. AES and RSA are well-known Encryption algorithms. Recent disclosures show that the NSA (National Security Administration) has found ways to crack existing internet Encryption algorithms (Matturdi, Zhou, Li, & Lin, 2015; Perlroth, Larson, & Shane, 2013). Cryptography is the art/science of secret writing (Karaarslan, Ergin, Turğut, & Kılıç, 2015). The most basic service that cryptography provides is encryption. Encryption converts data into a format (ciphertext) that only the intended recipients may read. The aim is to ensure confidentiality (Kaufman, Perlman, & Speciner, 2002).

In light of all this information, we conclude that data security must be ensured to ensure privacy. Problems arising from using data without privacy may leave individuals and companies in distress. Therefore, with several applications and changes to be made at both the technical and awareness level, it will be possible to protect privacy by providing data security awareness.

Relation of Data Security Issue with Digital Literacy and Communication Processes

The future of communication brings us to a point where there will be much more complex conditions, and communication will inevitably be at the center of life. Therefore, in such a case, it would be helpful to combine the data security and privacy discussed in the previous sections with the digital literacy issue in this section to explain the problem.

The more critical the privacy phenomenon is for people and companies, the more digital literacy becomes necessary to understand and realize this serious situation sustainably. Considering the 21st century, which is living under information bombardment, the uncontrolled circulation of information directly threatens privacy. Whereas all kinds of mass media, including new communication tools, especially the internet, have an essential role in transferring knowledge, they are the first source that individuals apply when they need information.

While information is power, conversely, it may become a tremendous threat when it is not used correctly. For this reason, the regular and controlled flow of information depends on the level of digital competencies and digital literacy in using technologies that transmit information. Media is where much information may circulate due to its nature and is partially devoid of control and supervision; these areas are where contradictory, incorrect, or distorted information is found. At the point reached today, it is possible to circulate misinformation and fake news on all media platforms. It makes the confirmation of the information necessary. In this context, we are faced with the importance of media literacy.

The prodigiousness and diversity of the information in the media and the fact that it may be inaccurate/fake make it arduous for the public to understand and analyze the data and simultaneously cause discombobulation. Thus, individuals may be manipulated in the information flow they are exposed to, become irate, and ineluctably experience situations that aliment the lynching culture.

In the period where digital transformation is proceeding; therefore, in such a period, literacy such as digital, media, and technology has become necessary for individuals, and information and communication are essential in terms of improving the daily needs of individuals and accessing the information they need in order to use their full potential (Horton, 2008). Nonetheless, the reliability of the information is possible with the correct use of information access tools. Otherwise, this situation may lead to some undesirable or criminal cases.

According to the Cost of Cybercrime Study (Ponemon-Institute, 2016), the cost of cybercrime for US organizations is 17.36 million dollars on average, 8.39 million dollars for organizations in Japan, and 7.84 million dollars for those in Germany. Security breaches may further affect end users. In some cases, FBI data becomes remarkable when this situation is reflected as a complaint. In 2015, the FBI received 288,012 complaints regarding cybercrime, with more than 40% of these complaints resulting in monetary losses (Cain, Morgan, & Still, 2018). As is known, cyber-security threats are a problem that affects not only institutions nonetheless individuals, and measures should be taken to prevent losses (Aslan, Aktaş, & Akbıyık, 2020).

Taking precautions depends on making some prognostications beforehand; categorical risks must be identified to make estimations, and actions must be taken accordingly. Risk communication, which includes disseminating information about all types of risks and hazards, is essential to developing a rational understanding of risks (Reynolds & Seeger, 2005, p. 47). In contrast, cyber-hygiene also draws attention as an effective solution besides identifying risks and managing the situation with an initiative-taking approach besides identifying risks and managing the situation with an initiative-taking approach, cyber-hygiene also draws attention as an effective solution. In the field of cyber security, that is, data security, the understanding of cyber-hygiene has come to the fore recently. Although cyber-hygiene is critical in protecting cyber-security, it should not be seen as synonymous with cyber-security. Cyber-hygiene involves establishing and maintaining healthy cyber behaviors (Vishwanath, et al., 2020), in other words, to protect individuals' financial and social information against cyber-attacks, individuals need to follow the rules and make these behaviors a habit. As the level of awareness and implementation of these rules and behaviors, called cyber-hygiene, increases, people's protection level against possible cyber-security violations will increase. No doubt, this will directly affect digital and media literacy competencies. Growing cyber threats make end-user computer security behavior even more critical because individuals consciously or unconsciously take action that uses cyber breaches (Bulgurcu, Cavusoglu, & Benbasat, 2009). Today, with the increasing number of cyber-crimes, governments, security experts, and decision-makers want individuals to give more importance to the issue of cyber-hygiene (Vishwanath, et al., 2020).

As indicated, the issue of data security is essential in terms of ensuring privacy, which is related to the level of *digital literacy* that will enable cyber-security measures to be taken. Therefore, increasing information contamination with the centralization of communication, media reading habits gaining importance, being unaffected by *fake news*, and overcoming the difficulties experienced in the virtual world, such as cyberbullying, can be possible by increasing digital literacy. Many platforms and systems often have security options that may be set and changed; nonetheless, end users often do not understand these options and know how to find and use them (Furnell, 2005).

CONCLUSION

The increasing number of communication technologies affects both individuals and businesses. Technological developments such as smartphones, tablets, laptop computers, wearable technologies, cyber-physical systems, autonomous robots, augmented reality technologies, and artificial intelligence, which are new every day, deepen digital transformation and accomplish more efficacious than the previous day. With the COVID-19 pandemic, which was experienced very soon and whose effect is still persistent, large masses have rapidly adopted digital transformation with its much more profound impact.

These possibilities, tremendous developments for the field of communication, on the one hand, have a say in the transition of humanity to the next stage; on the other hand, they have some systemic and human openings capable of shaking people to the deepest. With the increasing technological possibilities, more data production may pave the way for cybercrimes that expose and disclose the most private ones rather than their benefits and harm to individuals. Increasing numbers of misinformation activities confuse individuals and make it difficult to distinguish truth from delusiveness.

Information circulating uncontrolled similarly enhances the possibility of personal data falling into the hands of malware and individuals. While data security is under threat, we observe that what may be done about cyber-security is diversified. At the point of protection, storage, and processing of sensitive and non-sensitive data, it is necessary to act together with some legal regulations and software, systematic and practical applications.

However, the increase in digital literacy comes to the fore regarding providing cyber-security and data security. Digital literacy teaches us how to use these media tools. In parallel with this, it shows how we may use these tools more safely. Therefore, from the perspective of communication, one of the vital future discussion topics is the necessity of reading and using digital media tools correctly. Continuity of data security and communication processes is an essential element that will prevent cyber-crimes.

REFERENCES

Ala-Mutka, K. (2011). *Mapping digital competence: Towards a conceptual understanding*. Seville, Spain: European Commission, Joint Research Centre, Institute for Prospective Technological Studies. doi:10.13140/RG.2.2.18046.00322

Altun, A., Pembecioğlu, N., Orhon, E., Aydın, H., Erkmen, N., Şahin, G., Üstün, E. (2018). *Medya okuryazarlığı*. Ankara: Milli Eğitim Bakanlığı Publications.

Artut, S. (2014). *Teknoloji- insan birlikteliği*. Istanbul: Ayrıntı Publications.

Aslan, T., Aktaş, B., & Akbıyık, A. (2020). Kullanıcıların bilgisayar güvenliği davranışını inceleme: Siber Hijyen. *7. Uluslararası Yönetim Bilişim Sistemleri Konferansı"Sağlık Bilişimi ve Analitiği"*. İzmir. Retrieved from https://www.researchgate.net/profile/Tugce-Aslan-3/publication/348182462_kullanicilarin_bilgisayar_guvenligi_davranisini_inceleme_siber_hijyen/links/5ff2c5a6299bf140886c7412/kullanicilarin-bilgisayar-guvenligi-davranisini-inceleme-siber-hijyen.pdf

Aufderheide, P. (1993). Media literacy. A report of the national leadership conference on media literacy. *Communications and Society Program* (pp. 3-44). Washington, DC: Aspen Institute.

Bawden, D. (2008). Origins and Concepts of digital literacy. In C. Lankshear, & M. Knobel, *Digital literacies: Concepts, policies and practices* (pp. 17- 32). New York: Peter Lang.

Belshaw, D. A. (2011). What is digital literacy? A pragmatic investigation. *Ed.D Dissertation*. Department of Education, Durham University. Retrieved from http://etheses.dur.ac.uk/3446/

Bulgurcu, B., Cavusoglu, H., & Benbasat, I. (2009). Roles of information security awareness and perceived fairness in information security policy compliance. *European and Mediterranean Conference on Information Systems 2009*, (pp. 1-11). Izmir.

Cain, A. A., Morgan, E. E., & Still, J. D. (2018). An exploratory study of cyber hygiene behaviors and knowledge. *Journal of Information Security and Applications, 42*, 36-45. doi:10.1016/j.jisa.2018.08.002

Castells, M. (2011). A network theory of power. *International Journal of Communication, 5*, 773-787.

Ceylan, E. B., Demiryürek, E., & Kandemir, B. (2015). Sosyal ağlarda güncel güvenlik riskleri ve korunma yöntemleri. *Uluslararası Bilgi Güvenliği Mühendisliği Dergisi, 1*(1), 8-10.

Chewae, M., Hayikader, S., & M. H. Hasan, J. İ. (2015). How much privacy we still have on social network?. *International Journal of Scientific and Research Publications, 5*(1), 1-3.

Condy, J., Chigona, A., Gachago, D., & Ivala, E. (2012). Pre-Service students' perceptions and experiences of digital storytelling in diverse classrooms. *Turkish Online Journal of Educational Technology, 11*(3), 278-285.

Crowe, A. R. (2006). Technology, citizenship, and the social studies classroom: education for democracy in a technological age. *International Journal of Social Education, 21*(1), 111-121.

Dede, C. (2010). Comparing frameworks for 21st century skills. In J. Bellanca, & R. Brandt, *21st century skills: Rethinking how students learn* (pp. 51-76). Bloomington, IN: Solution Tree Press.

Dijk, J. V. (2016). *Ağ toplumu.* Istanbul: Kafka Publications.

Eshet-Alkalai, Y. (2004). Digital literacy: A conceptual framework for survival skills in the digital era. *Journal of Educational Multimedia and Hypermedia, 13*(1), 93-106.

Eshet-Alkalai, Y., & Amichai-Hamburger, Y. (2004). Experiments in digital literacy. *cyberpsychology & behavior, 7*(4), 421-429.

Eyüpoğlu, C., Aydın, M. A., Sertbaş, A., Zaim, A., & Öneş, O. (2017). Büyük veride kişi mahremiyetinin korunması. *Bilişim Teknolojileri Dergisi, 10*(2), 177-184. doi:10.17671/gazibtd.309301

Furnell, S. (2005). Why users cannot use security. *Computers & Security, 24*(4), 274-279.

Ghazinour, K., & Ponchak, J. (2017). Hidden privacy risks in sharing pictures on social media. *Procedia Computer Science, 113*, 267-272. doi:10.1016/j.procs.2017.08.367

Gündüz, M. Ş. (2022). Uluslararası hukuk açısından kişisel veri güvenliği. Batman: Batman Üniversitesi, Lisansüstü Eğitim Enstitüsü. (Published Master's Thesis).

Hague, C., & Payton, S. (2010). *Digital literacy across the curriculum.* Futurelab. Retrieved from https://www.nfer.ac.uk/publications/futl06/futl06.pdf

Herman, N. D., Maknun, J., Barliana, S., & Mardiana, R. (2019). Technology literacy level of vocational high school students. *Proceedings of the 5th UPI International Conference on Technical and Vocational Education and Training (ICTVET 2018)*, (pp. 519-522). doi:10.2991/ictvet-18.2019.118

Hobbs, R. (2010). *Digital and media literacy: A plan of action.* Washington, DC: The Aspen Institute. Retrieved from https://www.aspeninstitute.org/wp-content/uploads/2010/11/Digital_and_Media_Literacy.pdf

Honan, E. (2008). Barriers to teachers using digital texts in literacy classrooms. *Literacy, 42*(1), 36-43.

Horton, J. F. (2008). *Understanding information literacy: A primer.* Paris: United Nations Educational, Scientific and Cultural Organization-UNESCO. Retrieved from https://unesdoc.unesco.org/ark:/48223/pf0000157020

ITEEA. (2000). *Standards for technological literacy: Content for the study of technology.* Reston, VA: Iteea-International Technology and Engineering Educators Association.

JISC. (2014). *Developing digital literacies.* JISC: Joint Information Systems Committee. Retrieved from https://www.jisc.ac.uk/guides/developing-digital-literacies

Karaarslan, E., Ergin, A. M., Turğut, N., & Kılıç, Ö. (2015). Elektronik sağlık kayıtlarının gizlilik ve mahremiyeti. *Conference: INET-TR .* Istanbul. Retrieved from http://acikerisim.mu.edu.tr/xmlui/bitstream/handle/20.500.12809/9990/Karaarslan.pdf?sequence=3&isAllowed=y

Kaufman, C., Perlman, R., & Speciner, M. (2002). *Network security: Private communication in a public world.* Upper Saddle River, NJ: Prentice Hall.

Kurbanoğlu, S. (2010). Bilgi okuryazarlığı: Kavramsal bir analiz. *Türk Kütüphaneciliği, 24*(4), 723-747.

Kurt, A. A., Orhan, D., Yaman, F., Solak, M. Ş., & Türkan, F. (2014). Bilgi ve iletişim teknolojileri ışığında Türkiye'de yapılan okuryazarlık çalışmalarındaki eğilim. *Eğitim Teknolojileri Araştırma Dergisi, 5*(2), 1-21.

Küzeci, E. (2010). *Kişisel verilerin korunması.* Ankara: Turhan Kitapevi.

Leaning, M. (2019). An Approach to digital literacy through the integration of media and information literacy. *Media and Communication, 7*(2), 4-13.

Matturdi, B., Zhou, X., Li, S., & Lin, F. (2015). Big data security and privacy: A review. *China Communications, 11*(4), 135-145.

Newcomb, A. (2018, Mart 24). *A timeline of Facebook's privacy issues u* Retrieved from nbcnews.com: https://www.nbcnews.com/tech/social-media/timeline-facebook-s-privacy-issues-its-responses-n859651

Noujaim, J., & Amer, K. (Directors). (2019). *The Great Hack* [Motion Picture]. Retrieved from https://www.netflix.com/title/80117542

Oliver, R., & Towers, S. (2000). Benchmarking ICT Literacy In Tertiary Learning Settings. *Proceedings of the 17th Annual ASCILITE Conference,* (pp. 381-390).

Patel, M. (2017). Cyber security for social networking sites: Issues, challenges and solutions. *International Journal for Research in Applied Science & Engineering Technology (IJRASET), 5*(4), 833-838.

Perdana, R., Yani, R., Jumadi, J., & Rosana, D. (2019). Assessing students' digital literacy skill in senior high school Yogyakarta. *JPI-Jurnal Pendidikan Indonesia, 8*(2), 169-177. doi:10.23887/jpi-undiksha.v8i2.17168

Perlroth, N., Larson, J., & Shane, S. (2013, September 5). *NSA able to foil basic safeguards of privacy on web.* Retrieved from nytimes.com: https://www.nytimes.com/2013/09/06/us/nsa-foils-much-internet-encryption.html

Ponemon-Institute. (2016). *2016 cost of cyber crime study & the risk of business innovation.* Ponemon Institute.

Reynolds, B., & Seeger, M. W. (2005). Crisis and emergency risk communication as an integrative model. *Journal of Health Communication, 10,* 43-55.

Rogers, E. M. (2003). *Diffusion of innovations* (5th Edition ed.). New York: Free Press.

Şimşek, O. (2008). *Anayasa hukukunda kişisel verilerin korunması.* İstanbul: Beta Yayınları.

Vishwanath, A., Neo, L. S., Goh, P., Lee, S., Khader, M., Ong, G., & Chin, J. (2020). Cyber hygiene: The concept, its measure, and its initial tests. *Decision Support Systems, 128.* doi:10.1016/j.dss.2019.113160

PERSONAL DATA SECURITY IN SURVEILLANCE SOCIETY: AN ANALYSIS OF THE INTERNET IN TERMS OF PANOPTICON

*Sezgin SAVAŞ**
*Esra TUNÇAY***

INTRODUCTION

Whether the internet is a panopticon or not is debatable in today's world. While many scholars suggest that the internet reinforces surveillance, the others claim that it is a device of liberation. The internet offers certain structural opportunities for people to be free. Ideally, the internet is described as a space of liberation, participation, and sharing ideas. Indeed, the internet potentially offers these opportunities. Individuals stay in touch with each other, have access to public sphere, and can access to an immense amount of storage of knowledge like never before. However, it is necessary to discuss how these opportunities exist in practice and whether the internet is used for surveillance or not.

Jeremy Bentham's concept of panopticon is often referred to in the discussions related to the internet and surveillance. The concept of panopticon gained much popularity due to Foucault's adaptation of it into the social sciences. It became a central

* Assistant Professor, Gelisim University Faculty of Fine Arts, Communication Design Department, ssavas@gelisim.edu.tr

** Assistant Professor, American University of the Middle East, General Education Department esra.tuncay@aum.edu.kw

concept in new media studies. Whether the internet is a panopticon or not is an ongoing debate and the various concepts such as superpanopticon, sinopticon, polyopticon, omniopticon, and so on.

Surveillance can be discussed from various vantage points and in terms of many sample cases. Accordingly, there are numerous studies in the scholarship on surveillance and the internet. Çapar's (2019) study, which is on the perception of university students regarding internet surveillance, shows that university students are aware of the surveillance, consider it as a serious matter, and are worried about it. West and Bowman's (2016) study focuses on the ethical side of the surveillance of civilians, discussing the ethical expectations and issues regarding the use of unmanned aerial vehicles. The study attempts to explore the ethical dimensions of the issue from the perspective of classical philosophy and modern behavioural approaches. The study concludes that thanks to the unprecedented benefits of drones, they can be of great use for the public welfare notwithstanding the moral hazard they cause. The problem of moral hazard, the study argues, can be overcome by specifying the accountability, legislative provisions, and regulatory criteria of the use of unmanned aerial vehicles. Sewell (1998), in his study that suggests a new model of industrial labour process which maintains discipline under the circumstances of teamwork, offers a surveillance management system that represents "vertical" and "horizontal" forms of surveillance and that constitutes the fundamentals for the hybrid system to function in maintaining the control of workplace. Aydın's (2011) study, in which surveillance is viewed as a social problem, states that the internet has become widespread in working life because it helps information societies to access information in the fastest, cheapest, and easiest way. This, the study further argues, has increased the potential of surveillance. Reaching or accessing the information has turned into something vital for the information societies due to globalisation. Consequently, the boundaries of private life and working life intertwine and the above-mentioned tools serve the surveillance practices. The individuals who hope that they will have more freedom, therefore, end up imprisoned in a modern panopticon.

Whether the internet is a platform of surveillance or not is an important thing to discuss. The security of personal data is also something to explore. The meaning of being watched on the internet, of personal data being stored or of being under pressure in order not to leave the system should be explored. In today's world, people are unwillingly or, for the most part, voluntarily become a part of this surveillance mechanism and generously share their personal data. The data shared on the internet, whether voluntarily or not, are stored indefinitely and this has certain consequences for the individual. While some people think about what it means to share one's personal data on the internet and its potential consequences, most people do not. This shows that what surveillance means for the individual and the individual's perception of surveillance need to be put under scrutiny.

There are various studies on the improvement of data security in the scholarship. Milliff (2020) suggests a body of obligations/liabilities through which the practices of data security can be measured. Secondly, he elaborates on certain threats in terms of data security. Lastly, he proposes a range of incomprehensive data security practices to tackle different threats. Politou et al. (2018), in their study, explores the effects of General Data Protection Regulation's (GDPR) legal necessities of protecting personal data on EU soil on withdrawing consent, the right to be forgotten, and personal lifestyle. The study also discusses the consequences of implementing these applications, practicing new legal provisions, and the emerging necessities in the age of internet. Tatiana et al. (2022), on the other hand, dwells on data security and psychological safety in a study which analyses the factors that influence the changes occurring in the quality of education during the COVID-19 pandemic, which caused all educational institutions to switch to e-learning. The study, unlike the studies pursued before, student safety is not considered only as an extension of data security. Rather, it is viewed as something psychological and argued that psychological safety is influential on student participation and academic achievement. Macnish and Van der Ham's (2020) study discusses some of the ethical issues that the researches of cyber security face and criticises the governance in the ethics of cyber security by emphasising the shortcomings of the practices of governance. The study suggests that teaching ethics should be focused on more in the computer sciences. The study further argues that codes of conduct should be improved and made more widespread. Macnish and Van der Ham conclude that the scholarship of cyber security is in need of a new topic of discussion with regard to ethics.

The aim of this study, accordingly, is to discuss whether the internet is a surveillance mechanism or not, to find out for what purposes the obtained personal data can be used/is used, and explore what all these mean for the individual. Whereas the first chapter focuses particularly on the notions of personal data security and privacy, the second chapter dwells on surveillance society and the internet. The third chapter, on the other hand, put personal data under scrutiny within the context of surveillance society. The findings of the study suggest that the internet offers practical space for surveillance, going way beyond the boundaries of panopticon and differentiating itself in terms of its purposes.

Personal Data Security and Privacy

The emergence of the internet caused significant changes concerning the lives of people. Many activities held face-to-face before are now held online and many concepts regarding daily life are being reconsidered. It is a known fact that people share certain information with others within the process of carrying out their daily practices. Since this transmission of information occurs on an interpersonal level, it is rather unlikely to talk about an invasion of privacy.

However, things are a bit different in today's world. Thanks to the internet, people are now able to stay connected with each other (Çokluk, 2021, p. 363). Given that one's life is now integrated into the digital world, the personal information being shared is no longer on an interpersonal level. The information shared by an individual might end up in the hands of third parties with or without that individual's knowledge. This information can be obtained, stored, and used. The information can, for the most part, be used against the will of the individual. Therefore, the importance of the security of the personal data shared online becomes a major topic of discussion.

Personal data is a form of information which, directly or indirectly, leads to identification by referring to one's ID number or physical, physiological, mental, economic, cultural, and social identity (Romansky, 2017, p. 99). Personal data refers to all sorts of information about a real person. Amongst these information are location, likes, comments, and the device used (Çokluk Cömert, 2019, p. 166). An individual's name, ID number, location information as well as physical, genetic, mental, economic, and cultural aspects can be considered as data (Stepenko et al., 2022, p. 191-192). Personal data, accordingly, includes all information about a person.

The amount of personal data shared publicly by an individual grows each year. Thanks to all of the smart devices, more personal data can be collected and processed. Drawing a line, accordingly, between processing legitimate information and the privacy of private life gains much significance (Stepenko et al., 2022, p. 190-191). This has to do with the regulations regarding the protection of personal data online. Considering the importance of personal data, the existence of the regulations that restrict the collection of these data has become necessary.

The legislations regarding the protection of personal data usually follow the directives of OECD. According to the directives of OECD, there must be limitations put on the collection of personal data and the data must be obtained legally with the consent of the individual. The collected information must be up-to-date, correct, and complete. The purpose of obtaining information must be stated. The collected data must not be used for any other purpose. They must be protected with security measures. Policies and practices regarding personal data must be clear. The subjects of data have the right to obtain information about themselves and to object to the accuracy of data. The institution collecting personal information must be held accountable to the one providing the information (Cha&Yeh, 2018, p. 50511).

The fundamental principles of the protection of privacy are defined in the European Convention on Human Rights and the Convention for the Protection of Human Rights and Fundamental Freedoms, which entered into force in 1953. The protection of personal data turned into The Convention for the Protection of Individuals with Regard to Automatic Processing of Personal Data since 1981. In 1995, conversely, the managing bodies of United Nations accepted the Data Protection Directive 95/46/EC and the convention was replaced with General Data Protection Regulation (GDPR). In April 2016, General Data Protection Regulation (GDPR) which repealed the "Directive on protection of individuals with regard to the processing of personal data and on the free movement of such data and 95/46/EC" was accepted and put into effect in May 24th of 2018 after a transition period of two years. The regulation defines the new circumstances under which the personal data can be processed in the European Union. It does not require UN governments to make any changes on local laws and therefore is strictly binding. General Data Protection Regulation, on the other hand, is cross-border. This means that the provisions are applicable not only to the companies in UN but also to all persons and institutions that are interested in processing the personal data of UN citizens. The legislation, put it differently, states that technology should make the free of charge distribution of personal information easier within the boundaries of United Nations and should be distributed to the third world countries and international organisations on the condition that the personal data must be protected (Stepenko et al., 2022, p. 191).

Legislative regulations along with the developments in information technologies have increased the possibility of using the collected personal data against the owner of that data (Zharova&Elin, 2017, p. 482). Thanks to the developments in information technologies, organisations have acquired more personal data than ever via personalised services and ads (Cha&Yeh, 2018, p. 50510). Obtaining this much data have put the purposes of the use of digital data into question. Personal data can be obtained and used for various reasons. Individuals' perception of the use of personal data can be quite different as well.

It would not be wrong to say that people usually do not second-guess the reasons why certain information like phone number, driver's license number, and postcode are requested from us. Instead, they think that it would be beneficial to them if they shared the requested information (Bauman&Lyon, 2020, p. 142). This, however, might not be the case. Although the collected data make things easier in the digital world, it also means that some of the information that need to be kept are made public. This causes many threats to emerge in terms of personal data.

Online threats to personal data security have been discussed from various vantage points including viruses, spywares, phishing, cyberbullying, fraud, and identity theft (Kirkham et al., 2013, p. 12). These data not only allow third parties to obtain information about people but also make various illegal practices possible (Zhang, 2018, p. 275). Personal data, whether shared voluntarily or not, may affect one's life in future. The internet never forgets, so information once shared can be used for fraud, bullying etc. in future. This means that the individual is always digitally in danger. Furthermore, personal data can be used by other purposes than ill-intentioned third parties.

Personal data have monetary value, but people usually are not aware of that. This state of unawareness leads people to underestimate the economic potential of their personal data and to let their digital identities become commodity (Malgieri&Custers, 2018, p. 290). These data have considerable commercial value for the internet service providers and their collection and analysis cause risk to privacy (Zhang, 2018, p. 275). Privacy risks, therefore, are not posed only by third parties. The notion of transparency that the internet embodies is itself a threat to privacy (Kirkham et al., 2013, p. 12). The concepts such as privacy and surveillance, accordingly, are major points of discussion here.

Digital privacy can be approached from five perspectives: (1) some of the governments' disposition to collect personal data in order to maintain political security, (2) organisations' disposition to collect personal data for financial purposes, (3) sociologically ill-intentioned actors' disposition to use the personal data created in social networks, (4) whether the personal data should be kept in the organisation's own database or in the user's own safekeeping mechanisms, (5) the analysis of the legislations on the protection of personal data. In today's digitalised society, privacy is one of the major problems. In addition to sharing personal information, privacy should be discussed in terms of surveillance and discipline. In the age of data, the problem of data security is not just about privacy in the conventional sense. It leads to the analysis and investigation of people's data as well as to the prediction of their behaviour (Zhang, 2018, p. 275). In other words, what is being at stake here is not only an assessment of people's present but also of their future. Personal data, accordingly, are of great importance in terms of surveillance, discipline, and predicting future behaviour.

Surveillance Society and The Internet

The concept of surveillance has been historically considered in terms of supporting the power of the states and viewed as a tool of social discipline. Historically speaking, surveillance has always existed in each time of period. The traces of surveillance can be found in people's interest in each other's states as well as in people morally overseeing each other (Lyon, 2013, p. 86). The practices of surveillance can be historically analysed in three stages: (1) primitive communities, feudal societies, empires, and so on that can be defined as pastoral surveillance. Such practices as overseeing the work force, possessing tax rolls, maintaining the control of nomadic life, combat readiness, and population census are the mechanisms that make this kind of surveillance work. (2) The second stage, which can be described as technical surveillance, occurred with the emergence of modern societies. This system prioritises bureaucracy in public sphere and scientific management in production in order to reinforce the power of the state and maintain social discipline. (3) The third stage, namely informatics surveillance, views daily life both as individual surveillance and mass surveillance. In this stage, in which technological devices are used and the power's need to 'know' is on the rise, the internet holds an important place (Tümurtürkan, 2010, p. 5).

Surveillance is defined as the act of watching a suspect or the area where a crime will possibly be committed (Oxford, n.d; Cambridge, n.d). Today, however, surveillance is discussed in a much broader sense. The term can no longer be considered only in terms of crime or the possibility of a crime being committed. It now encompasses all human life. Surveillance has been included in social sciences especially as a part of the technological developments. Many studies that refer to surveillance have been conducted and the first person to talk about the idea of a computer-based surveillance society is Gary T. Marx (Marx, 1985). Marx (1985) broadened the scope of the concept of surveillance in modern society.

Although the concept of surveillance is as old as the history of humanity, the notion of surveillance which refers to a structure in which every bit of information is used by the power can be historically considered a new concept (Tümurtürkan, 2010, p. 4). Surveillance society is not limited only to recording footages of people by camera surveillance system, use of shopping cards, and swiping cards to access workplace. All of these established electronic systems, which are basically the devices of collecting and processing personal data, indicate a much more complex structure and this structure, in its essence, is indicative of the way that the world operates in the twenty-first century (Lyon, 2013, p. 86).

Whether the internet is a platform of surveillance or not is an ongoing topic of discussion in today's world. Whereas for some the internet solely provides a space of freedom, for others the internet does nothing but to consolidate discipline. Conceptually, the discussion of whether the internet is a tool of surveillance or not is now being approached from the vantage point of Jeremy Bentham's architectural model of panopticon.

The various concepts such as superpanopticon, sinopticon, polyopticon, and omniopticon often appear in the scholarship in addition to the concept of panopticon. Etymologically speaking, the word panopticon was originated from the Greek words "pan" and "optikón", meaning "all seeing" (Bauman&Lyon, 2020, p. 22, 67). Panopticon can be visualised as follows: there is a watchtower in the centre. The building is divided into cells, which are arranged along the external wall. Cells have two small windows: whereas one faces towards the watchtower in the middle of the building, the other faces the outside with a view to the sky. Placing one guard into the watchtower and one prisoner inside the cell is sufficient for panopticon to function properly. The prisoners can be seen in silhouettes from the watchtower due to the light. This eliminates the possibility of hiding in the dark and thus reverses the principle of the dungeon (Foucault, 2015, p. 86). Being in the light and being constantly monitored are much more repressive than being in the dark. Visibility turns into a trap (Foucault, 1992, p. 251).

The idea of deterrence is vital for panopticon. Being in a state of constant surveillance by a guard eliminates the thought of doing evil. Panopticon is cheaper than most of the other prison models. There is no need for guns and violence. The gaze of the one who sees all from the watchtower is internalised by all of the prisons and this makes the entire system to function. This form of power is sustainable and cheaper. But it would be wrong to say that power is exercised by a single person in panopticon. Panopticon includes everyone: the ones who exercise power and the ones who are subject to this exercise of power (Foucault, 2015, p. 94-96). Panopticon is characterised by the visibility of one side and the invisibility of the other. The ones who are constantly monitored can never be sure whether they are actually being monitored or not. They, therefore, always act as if they are being watched. The whole point is to make the threat of punishment felt by the prisoners at all times to maintain discipline. The idea is to show that one can never remain hidden and misbehaviour will never remain unpunished (Bauman, 2006, p. 42-43, 58).

There is no room for any place that is devoid of surveillance in panopticon (Bauman, 2006, p. 58). Panopticon functions through visibility, which makes power function. Even though surveillance is a discontinuous process, it includes continuity. Bentham's starting point was that although the power is visible, it is unverifiable. Even though the watchtower physically exists, there is no way to know for sure that there is indeed a guard in it, monitoring everyone.

In order to make sure that the presence of the observer remain unverified, Bentham envisaged venetian blinds on the windows and partitions which intersected the hall at right angles as well as zig-zag openings instead of doors in order to pass from one quarter to the other. The slightest noise, a gleam of light, a brightness in a half-opened door would give away the presence of the observer (Foucault, 1992, p. 252-253). "He who is subjected to a field of visibility, and who knows it, assumes responsibility for the constraints of power; he makes them play spontaneously upon himself" (Foucault, 1995, p. 202)

In panopticon, each prisoner is seen by the observer but the prisoners cannot communicate with one another. The side walls prevent them from coming into contact with one another. The prisoner becomes an object of information, but can never be a subject in communication (Foucault, 1992, p. 252). Panopticon, accordingly, is a technology of power that aims to solve the problem of surveillance. Although this innovation was used during the entire eighteenth century, procedures of power are greater in number and richer in content in modern society (Foucault, 2015, p. 87). The reason why the inmates cannot move in panopticon is that they are in a state of constant surveillance. There is no room for defiance or non-compliance, for the whereabouts of the guards roaming freely inside the building is unknown. Today, however, this immobility is no more and we are in a post-panoptic age. In the post-panoptic age, the majority of the information are collected by the private organisations through the individual's use of cell phone, visit to a shopping mall, having fun, surf in the internet or travel (Bauman&Lyon, 2020, p. 22-24). While panopticon restricts the movement of the prisoner, it makes it easier for the guard to move around. The guard, however, does not disappear altogether and sometimes has to make his/her presence visible. Panopticon was an expensive project and the inspector was responsible for the lives of the inmates. In today's world, conversely, observers and inspectors can disappear. This means that the relationship of dependence between the prisoner and the inspector is no more, and mobility and nomadism are on the rise (Bauman&Lyon, 2020, p. 14-15).

Now that the power is equipped with all sorts of technologies, walls and windows become useless. In today's world, the observed and the observed are intertwined, and surveillance takes place throughout one's life. The forms of surveillance that are applicable to daily activities, everyday shopping, the state of using the internet, and the use of social media get increasingly common (Bauman&Lyon, 2020, p. 11-15). Surveillance is part of many daily online activities. Many people are now aware of the fact that surveillance is one of the most important topics to discuss in today's world and it has certain consequences for their lives (Bauman&Lyon, 2020, p. 11).

In order to understand the meaning of surveillance as accurately as possible, one has to understand the dimensions of data processing. Thanks to the internet, considerable amount of physical and non-physical data can be included in databases (Bauman&Lyon, 2020, p. 12, 19). These data can be processed and analysed when necessary. It is safe to say that the possibility to collect data through the active and passive traces of the users without getting the consent of the users is increasing as well as the size of the data collected.

Considering the technological potentialities, it can be observed that the notions of privacy and transparency are intermingled with the power relations. Whereas people make all the information about themselves transparent through their thoughts and actions, the presence of sovereign gains further invisibility. The internet, which can be identified as a mechanism of discipline, make people alienated from the real world and leads to isolation, whereas at the same time making possible for third parties to access personal information (Dolgun, 2004, p. 62-63). These personal information and profile can be used for various reasons. It is, therefore, significant to investigate what it means to obtain the personal information of individuals. Even though they are aware of the fact that they are being monitored, people generously share information about themselves without having any second thoughts. However, it is important to discuss the consequences of sharing, storing, and using this information in terms of security.

Personal Data Security in Terms of Surveillance Society

It is safe to suggest that knowledge in modern society is an important need to satisfy. From a managerial perspective, the information obtained about people is significant in terms of productivity and efficiency for the government and organisations. The concept of surveillance is of considerable importance to establish a state of possessing knowledge (Çankaya&Ekiz,

2018, p. 146). It is possible to obtain personal data through the surveillance of an individual.

The driving force behind surveillance is security. Security is the most fundamental driving force in terms of surveillance. The most basic justification of surveillance is that it maintains security (Bauman&Lyon, 2020, p. 114-115). Whether the individuals consent to surveillance or not is discussed in terms of security. The legitimacy of surveillance is grounded on the idea that surveillance is being done in order to protect the one who is being monitored. However, this suggestion brings forth the problem of privacy.

Personal data are part of the sense of socialisation. One cannot, for instance, have an identity card without giving his/her fingerprints first. Similarly, one needs to provide cell phone number and address information in order to do online shopping. All of this information are stored and used by third parties for advertising, promotion, and so on. It is not possible to make use of these services without giving consent and this means that one allows his/her data to be processed (Atagün, 2019, p. 21). It is, accordingly, safe to say that individuals are impelled to share their personal data so that they can go on living and continue to exist in the system.

Request to collect personal data is not just made by the governments today. For a long period of time, the right of privacy had prevented that request to be made. With the emergence of the internet, however, the boundaries of the right of privacy have become blurred. In the past, people could keep the information about their age, property ownership, record, and so on to themselves. Thanks to the internet, however, this information and much more have begun to be stored in the databases belonging to public and private institutions (Çankaya&Ekiz, 2018, p. 147). The stored information can be used whenever necessary and thus the individual has no say in it.

Some people are worried about the collected information about themselves. The personal data collected and stored by the governments, insurance companies, employers, banks, and marketing companies are worrisome (Bauman, 2006, p. 60). The collected and stored personal information can be used for advertising and promoting consumption. Practices such as content personalisation indicate how common collecting and storing personal data is. Such information allow third parties to know the individual better and thus leads to new ways of using the collected data. Within the context of consumerism, surveillance functions more loosely. Surveillance becomes much more widespread and common due to the marketing of technology companies (Bauman&Lyon, 2020, p. 13).

Thanks to the docile cooperation of people, service providers know people better than they know themselves. This intervention is even seen as a friendly helping hand. One can even argue that people live happily ever after in 'filter bubbles' (Bauman&Lyon, 2020, p. 137-142). With each connection, users create a filter bubble (Pariser, 2011). This refers to the conceptualisation of echo chamber in the sense of one-sided flow of information (Sunstein, 2009). This enables one to be situated in a homogeneous social environment constituted based on his/her likes, thoughts, and desires, where s/he is with alike-minded people.

The internet alters the perception of surveillance. Now everything is open to public consumption. Due to the social media, cell phone cameras, and free online video platforms, the boundaries between what is public and what is private are no longer clear. In today's world, panoptic nightmare turns into the promise of not being alone or isolated as well as of the desire of being noticed by others, and thus suppresses the other fears. Being watched and seen have become tempting rather than being a threat. Since it is believed that danger is everywhere, people have become addicted to surveillance and the visibility of surveillance (Bauman&Lyon, 2020, p. 36, 37, 119). Although some people are worried about the violation of private life, many others do not make a big deal out of it. Sharing personal information is not seen as something wrong, regardless of the organisation with which the information is being shared.

Because security is concerned with the future, the anticipated events are attempted to be overseen by the predictions based on digital techniques and statistics (Bauman&Lyon, 2020, p. 16). People do not immediately face the consequences of security/privacy violations and thus do not think about them often. The collected data through surveillance, however, are concerned with one's future as much as with one's present. The personal data obtained today can be used at any time in future. Stored personal data can be used in future in the ways that seem unimaginable today. Various third parties can make prospective arrangements in terms of the collected personal data.

In today's world, however, surveillance is not conducted directly. It is conducted indirectly through information. Therefore, one cannot simply explain surveillance only in terms of panopticon in today's world. It is a matter of considerable depth. The aim of surveillance is to turn people into consumers rather than to discipline them (Güven, 2014, p. 97-98). Panopticon still exists today and it is now powerful thanks to the technological developments (Bauman&Lyon, 2020, p. 70).

Surveillance is all around us nowadays. Private space as well as many information that need to be private have become public. Even the very possibility of protecting personal data is questionable now, for the majority of one's personal data are devoid of protection and security. Protecting personal data prevents one from carrying out many activities and practices. In other words, people are impelled to share their personal information voluntarily. What needs to be discussed, accordingly, is not whether the internet is a tool of surveillance or not but how much the internet actually enlarges the scope of surveillance. Although the internet has a liberating and ideal nature, it is obvious that the internet is something quite problematic in terms of sharing personal data.

CONCLUSION

With the development of the internet, the practices of surveillance have come to hold a significant place in people's lives. More than what is collected or the potential consequences, the constant state of being monitored is one of the defining characteristics of modern society. The reason behind the idea of surveillance should also be put under scrutiny. In the past, surveillance was conducted by the sovereign to establish citizenship consciousness, to repress the uprising, to keep people in check, and so on. Today, however, it has become a really complex mechanism. Many studies show that surveillance now has to do with consumption above all.

The major topic of discussion related to surveillance today is the collection of people's personal data. Personal data have become a field of interest for various public and private organisations due to the notion of consumption. Today's consumer society associates everything with consumption. People's personal data, accordingly, are used to better incorporate people into the system of consumption. To illustrate, the active and passive footprints that people leave behind on the internet allow profiles to be created and these profiles are used to offer personalised products and services. This is one of the most important consequences of surveillance.

Apart from the very presence of surveillance, it is also necessary to examine the perception of surveillance. People are in a position today where they have to share their personal information voluntarily in order to carry out many activities or practices. People are requested to give consent to share personal information just to be able to conduct even the simplest of everyday activities and if they refuse to do so, they are prevented from getting the necessary services. That being the case, even if they are worried about sharing their personal information, most of the people have inevitably become insensitive about it. This means the normalisation of personal data turning into public property as well as the disappearance of the idea that private information needs to remain private.

When one considers the consequences of surveillance in terms of personal data, one realises that the whole matter is, in fact, concerned with the problem of privacy. Many people today share personal information about themselves without having any second thoughts. Even the ones who are worried about sharing their personal data eventually give in. Even if the shared personal data do not have any immediate consequences for the individual, it must be remembered that once shared, the personal data remains on the internet forever and thus can be used for various purposes in future.

Perhaps, then, it would be better to explore the meaning of surveillance as a whole or people's perception of surveillance rather than examining whether the internet is a tool of surveillance or not. In today's world, surveillance technologies have improved considerably and thus the devices used in surveillance have become varied. This has altered the very meaning and purpose of surveillance as well as the perception of people in terms of surveillance. To conclude, in other words, surveillance has been integrated into modern life and has become diversified concerning its objectives.

REFERENCES

Atagün, Ö. F. (2019). *Gözetim toplumunda kişisel verilerin korunması*. Retrieved on 05 19, 2022, from https://www.omeratagun.com/files/Kisisel%20Verilerin%20Korunmas%C4%B1.pdf

Aydın, N. (2011). *Çalışma yaşamında özgürlük sorunu: Gözetim ve mahremiyetin yeni sınırları*. Karadeniz Teknik Üniversitesi Sosyal Bilimler Enstitüsü (Published Master's Thesis).

Bauman, Z. (2006). *Küreselleşme*. Istanbul: Ayrıntı Publications.

Bauman, Z. & Lyon, D. (2020). *Akışkan gözetim*. İstanbul: Ayrıntı Publications.

Cha, S. C. & Yeh, K. H. (2018). *A data-driven security risk assessment scheme for personal data protection*. IEEE Access, 6, 50510-50517.

Cambridge (n.d). *Surveillance*, Retrieved on 05 18, 2022 fromhttps://dictionary.cambridge.org/tr/s%C3%B6zl%C3%BCk/ingilizce/surveillance

Çankaya, H. & Ekiz, C. (2018). Biyopolitik açıdan kişisel verilerin korunmasi. *Memleket Siyaset Yönetim*, 13(29), 135-156.

Çapar, Z. B. (2019). *Üniversite öğrencilerinin internet gözetimine yönelik farkındalığı.* Anadolu Üniversitesi Sosyal Bilimler Enstitüsü (Published Master's Thesis).

Çokluk N. (2021). Bilgi çağında siyasi varlık olarak büyük veri tactical tech'in 'data and politics' projesi üzerine bir inceleme. Nil Çokluk (Ed.). In *Bilgi Çağında Siyaset* (p. 363-398). Ankara: Nobel Publications.

Çokluk Cömert, N. (2019). Bilgi egemen olmaktır: Dijital teknolojilerin siyasal iletişim çalışmalarında önemi. Oğuz Göksu (Ed.) In *İletişimin Dijital Boyutu* (p. 165-196). Konya: Literatürk.

Dolgun, U. (2004). Gözetim toplumunun yükselişi: Enformasyon toplumundan gözetim toplumuna. *Yönetim Bilimleri Dergisi,* 2(1), 55-74.

Foucault, M. (1992). *Hapishanenin doğuşu.* Ankara: İmge Publications.

Foucault, M. (1995). *Discipline and punish.* New York: Vintage Books.

Foucault, M. (2015). *İktidarın gözü.* Istanbul: Ayrıntı Publications.

Güven, O. Ö. (2014). Gözetim tekniklerinin güç ilişkileri bağlamında dönüşümü ve toplumsal denetim. *Atatürk İletişim Dergisi,* (7), 79-112.

Kirkham, T., Winfield, S., Ravet, S., Kellomäki, S. (2013). The personal data store approach to personal data security. *IEEE security & privacy,* 11(5), 12-19.

Macnish, K. & Van der Ham, J. (2020). Ethics in cybersecurity research and practice. *Technology in Society,* 63, 1-10.

Malgieri, G., and Custers, B. (2018). Pricing privacy–the right to know the value of your personal data. *Computer Law & Security Review,* 34(2), 289-303.

Milliff, A. (2020) Data security in practitioner-academic partnerships: An agenda for improvement. *MIT Political Science Department Research Paper No. 2020-6.*

Marx, G. T. (1985). The threat of 1984-style techniques. *The futurist,* June, 21-26.

Lyon, D. (2013). Gözetim toplumu. *Sosyologca,* (6), 85-99.

Oxford (t.y). *Surveillance,* Retrieved on 05 18, 2022 from https://www.oxford-learnersdictionaries.com/definition/english/surveillance

Pariser, E. (2011). *The filter bubble: What the internet is hiding from you.* United Kindom: Penguin Books.

Politou, E., Alepis, E., Patsakis, C. (2018). Forgetting personal data and revoking consent under the GDPR: Challenges and proposed solutions. *Journal of Cybersecurity,* 4(1), 1-20

Romansky, R. (2017). A survey of digital world opportunities and challenges for user's privacy. *International Journal on Information Technologies and Security,* 4(9), 97-112.

Stepenko, V., Dreval, L., Chernov, S., Shestak, V. (2022). EU personal data protection standards and regulatory framework. *Journal of Applied Security Research,* 17(2), 190-207.

Sunstein, C. R. (2009). *Going to extreems: How like and unite and divide.* New York: Oxford University Press.

Sewell, G. (1998). The discipline of teams: The control of team-based industrial work through electronic and peer surveillance. *Administrative Science Quarterly,* 43(2): 397-428.

Tatiana, B., Kobicheva, A., Tokareva, E., Mokhorov, D. (2022). The relationship between students' psychological security level, academic engagement and performance variables in the digital educational environment. *Education and Information Technologies*, 27, 9385–9399

Tümurtürkan, M. (2010). Gündelik hayatın gözetimi: "Panoptikon toplumu". *Ethos: Felsefe ve Toplumsal Bilimlerde Diyaloglar*, 2(3), 1-19.

West, J. P. & Bowman, J. S. (2016). The domestic use of drones: An ethical analysis of surveillance issues. *Public Administration Review*, 76(4), 649-659.

Zhang, D. (2018). Big data security and privacy protection. In 8th International Conference on Management and Computer Science (ICMCS), 77. Atlantis Press, 275-278.

Zharova, A. K. & Elin, V. M. (2017). The use of big data: A Russian perspective of personal data security. *Computer Law & security review*, 33(4), 482-501.

METAVERSE:
REAL DATA IN THE VIRTUAL UNIVERSE

*Kemal DENİZ**

INTRODUCTION

Throughout their recorded history, human beings have constantly developed inventions to make life easier. Since the Abacus, which is the most basic computing device, and The Antikythera Mechanism, which is known utilized in Ancient Greece as a mechanical astronomy computing device that is accepted to be the first example of a computer, people have needed to calculate data using devices and organize their lives accordingly. Even in ancient times, people had to count and process data, though they were not aware of its importance and value as we are today. If we exclude wars, the exploitation, and oppression of people executed against each other, civilizations that could at least comprehend the crucial requirements and manage to organize their social life accordingly, continued to develop and survive. That is due to the ability to use the scientific knowledge efficiently that has been going on since prehistoric times. In short, benefiting from the data that life offers us functionally has contributed to the development of humanity and civilization in one way or another throughout human history.

In the past decades, rapid advances in technology have been observed. Compared to today, from the years when a very small amount of data could be processed and stored in larger computer

---

* Assistant Professor, Munzur University Communication Faculty Radio, Television and Cinema Department. kedeniz@gmail.com

systems, we have reached the times when we begin to become familiar with the concepts of Artificial Intelligence, Augmented Reality, Virtual Reality, Machine Learning, Internet of Things, Data Mining, Meta Data, Data Processing, etc. The data technology we reach goes even further. With the concept of the Internet of Behaviors (IoB), individuals' behaviors in digital interactions are transformed into systematic data, and new behavioral models are developed for them and presented to them again through the digital world they engage in (Nyman, 2021a; Nyman, 2020). In the coming years, time will tell if an IoB for a better world and social life emerges from the results of data analyses based on the behavior of individuals and if smarter cities and urban life are formed. The concept of the Internet of Thoughts, or what neuroscientists call B/CI stands for Human Brain/Cloud Interface, (*see*, Spataro et al., 2022; Opris et al., 2021; Das et al., 2019; Martins et al., 2019), which connects brain cells to massive cloud-computing networks in real-time, is expected to be achievable by the end of the century. If research on this topic continues to advance at the current pace, the concept of integrating cloud technology with people's brains could become a reality in the coming decades. Still there are intense security concerns on privacy and security of Brain Data (*see* Vidal, 2022). It must be possible to guarantee the privacy and security of brain data.

Compared to the overall technological evolution of the world, reaching the times when the digital culture was constructed by a technological transformation in which these developments became a part of daily life and integrated with the people, took place before too many years passed. Rapidly developing information and data science technologies have made it inevitable for us to continue our existence in a world where digitalization transforms all concrete reality into data and virtualizes it. According to this notion, digital transformation has necessitated the reorganization of not only the people themselves but also all living and non-living beings and phenomena on the planet. Human, of course, was not late in taking the leading role in this crucial duty.

With the emergence of technological possibilities that can produce high amounts of data at an unimaginable speed before, both individuals with devices that can connect to the network they use in their daily practices, which include all data technology, and establishments that have to provide all the institutional organization necessary for the maintenance of social life, reproduce this data over and over again. All individuals and organizations worldwide linked to the network send data via massive fiber optic cables beneath the oceans (*see,* Cables, 2022; Submarine Cable Map 2020; Cable Data, 2014) and store it in data centers usually situated in deserts (Steers, 2022; Berry, 2021; Sperling, 2009). Furthermore, as Microsoft's underwater data center experiment shows (Christian, 2020; Haranas, 2020), data will be stored under the sea in the following years.

Of course, states, commercial companies, and all institutions and organizations that constantly collect our data "for our own benefit" continue to be the more organized elements of this process that operate in line with particular interests. In an era where so much data is stored in the clouds, it is a very natural impulse for people to be concerned about the privacy and secrecy of their data. The significance and value of privacy also seem to continue to be a topic of discussion as individuals continue to make themselves more public on the network.

The more visible we are on the networks, the more networks know about us. That is how networks offer more data specific to us in order to get more information about us. Thus, we continue to work to increase the data richness of the network in an inextricable cycle, and we produce and share private data with others, which will encourage new data production by others in the network. It appears to be a never-ending loop. This process actually manipulates our behavior patterns such as habit, attitude, response, or unresponsiveness and ignorance not only as data we share directly online but also in our tendencies, approaches, and reactions towards worldly facts. That circumstance triggers individuals to become reconstructed by the digital world.

While technology transforms the forms of organization in social, cultural life, and economic processes, individuals are transforming into more digitalized identities, in other words, digital-selves. Although their existential realities are not significantly detached from the actualities of the material world, their presence on the digital world is becoming increasingly concrete. Specifically, since Gen Z, those digitalized identities rebuild themselves socially, culturally, and existentially in this virtual universe, just as they produce their data. Furthermore, Gen Alphas (post-Millennials) were born directly into this technological transformation. Therefore, it can be predicted that the digital self will be more developed, as the biological growth of the alpha generation will continue to draw closer parallels to the advancement of technology.

Either a utopia or a dystopia environment where the importance of data goes beyond purely material reality also requires discussion on the concept of the Metaverse, which is too deep a subject to understand digitalized virtual universe concept. The digitalized data brought by technology has the capacity to reproduce, copy and record everything virtually. This situation removes the existing concrete reality of the universe which has formed over billions (13.84 billion) of years ontologically and places it in a new concept: A meta-universe.

Will the human self, which has already converted into the digital self in the present, be a meta-self in the future, leaving its existential human being nature that has been growing with its own specific ontology for 300,000 years and continuing to adapt to this non-meta-universe? What kind of human self and existence will the Metaverse reveal, and what will be the prominence and value of digital data in the context of this entity? The continuation of an entity in another ontological environment may also show that its ontology in its essence in real world is already problematic. Likewise, if the human being is already destroying this structure in the real world, how the ontology of the human with the meta-self in the meta-universe could appear? Could such a being really exist in the near or far future? Should that be called a posthuman? Aside from the aforementioned, would the individual's entire self become the "one's own data" that comprise that being in the Metaverse? If it has not already happened in today's digital world by now!

These all should not be mind-blowing questions! Besides, these questions and their answers should not prevent asking: "Will it contributes to the understanding of the world in a more ideal or at least livable worldliness in the relationship between the Metaverse and the individual?" Especially at the time of writing this chapter, when the concept of the Metaverse is widespread, being able to think about these questions and evaluate perspectives for the future will allow us to take pleasure in swaying on a virtuality - reality swing.

Data Science and Big Data

In Gartner's *Top Strategic Technology Trends for 2022*, they argue that 12 trends will be shaping the future of "digital business" until the end of 2025. All of them are related to data, including its management, security, and optimization for benefiting from it in digital business (Groombridge, 2022). The data issue, whose importance is increasing continuously, is multidimensional. First, it has an aspect related to very complex technical and technological processes. This aspect of course, concerns the working field of data scientists. The other one is the social dimension of data. What do we understand from this? Since ancient times, people have needed data. Whatever the technological development background of the period they lived in, they generated methods to obtain these data. They tried to record, classify and use the data they had in a way that would provide various benefits both in daily life practices and in more complex and technical fields by performing certain operations.

Undoubtedly, just as all the scientific and technical inventions and efforts that contribute to the development of human history evolved to a different dimension with digitalization, "data" gained a different meaning and extent in the era when it could be digitized and processed in computer systems. Thus, it became the leading actor in a field called data science. Data science, which can be seen as a cause and a result of the rapid development of computer and information technologies in the modern age, started to develop in the 1960s. Before reaching its current level, data science spent its first crawling and walking stages with the work of the pioneers such as John Tukey, Chien Fu Jeff Wu, Peter Naur, Chikio Hayashi, and last but not least, William S. Cleveland (Press, 2013; Cao, 2017; Donoho, 2017).

The circumstance that data came to the agenda of the ordinary people was thanks to the fact that it found more place for itself in the triangle of society, culture, and economy. With the global spread of the Internet, computer-based devices based on digital data processing, the need for institutions to process information, and especially in the Internet 2.0 era's interaction possibilities brought to the users, digital data has become one of the most valuable assets. In a time when data has become so valuable, the technology utilized to apply data science varies by company or institution. The larger the company or the amount of data being handled, the more complicated the technological ecosystem supporting data science operations. (Kelleher & Tirney, 2018, p. 69). It is not a coincidence that we frequently hear the words, such as "whoever controls data will have control over the world in the future". Experts who understand the importance of data or people who think about this subject are not wrong to emphasize that data is the most valuable asset of the future, as well as today it is. Accordingly, in what context is data such crucial at this level? The answer is "Big Data".

Big data goes beyond the size of data that simply includes basic information about the individual. Therefore, it is necessary to consider big data as a concept those organizations like corporate, interagency, communities, companies, and governments process huge amounts of data in line with their own purposes and interests in a way to obtain meaningful results. Data should be collected regularly from various information sources and linked to other systems and platforms; uniform reporting standards should be established and any information should be completed to ensure accuracy and completeness. Finally, assessing the skills and profiles needed to extract value from data, designing efficient data value chains, and establishing appropriate procedures are two critical issues. A good internal data management system paired with a well-designed golden record can help solve the multi-layer login issue (Corea, 2019, p. 7).

When we look at it from an individual standpoint in the digital cultural landscape, data can be understood as bits of information obtained from activities related to all behavior and usage information created by the traces left by people using various smart devices, sharing on networks, and being in digital environments, etc. The data of each individual might obtained from various digital data collectors. It should pass through numerous distinct classifications, analyses, statistics, and correlations to provide valuable and applicable results from this data. In other words, the result should be a reasonable conclusion and a profitable evaluation acquired from the data analysis. Hence, the behaviors and user characteristics of individuals are classified and processed. Institutions and companies that grasp generalizations about individuals by correlations and predictions created from their digital traces proceed based on that data when designing and providing products and services. In particular, institutions and corporations take extensive action in response to data correlations and predictions. However, some researchers (*see* Bal, 2021; Chun, 2021; Marr, 2015) have brought a critical perspective to correlational data analysis.

Data Security

In the context of data security, the traces that individuals leave on the environment, applications, or devices to which they connect to the internet are crucial. It would be a very innocent approach to consider that these traces are simply obtained without their own knowledge and awareness and that these acquired data are used as feedback that can be used in the R&D, production, and supply of new services. If those who dominate the data can dominate the world, that is, the economy, and therefore people, then it is necessary to evaluate the concerns about the security of this data.

As technology continues to advance rapidly, ordinary people try to overcome the complexity of these constantly upcoming inventions and novelties by adapting these innovations to their individual, social and cultural life. Thus, they take the concerns about personal data security to the background and use this innovation as a tool to facilitate their essential daily practices. For that reason, they do not question what happens to their data any further. The fact that the data security issue has a technical dimension and cannot be perceived by the ordinary user well enough may be a reasonable explanation for that phenomenon. However, the presence of Global IT companies and governments, as well as the fact that large masses who do not have a high level of citizenship awareness that is why do not have an idea of what their rights are, make the data insecurely accessible to third parties and allow them to use it as they wish.

As social anthropologists say, a person has the physical and mental capacity to be "friends" in real life with a maximum of 150 people (Dunbar, 1992), while s/he can have thousands of friends on social networks. Thus, virtual data produced by people on social media are constantly shared with those networks of friends. We store almost any of our important data on devices that process and store digital data or, thanks to cloud technology, on servers. More precisely, they are storing the data we sent them on our behalf. Therefore, now we form an organic bond with data storage environments where, if not biologically, but culturally and as a daily life practice because of our inability to store all the information of life, or our minds that we have consciously or unconsciously made lazy.

Most of us do not memorize the phone numbers, email addresses, or even the home addresses of our closest relatives. We just digitally store very important and necessary information for ourselves. Imagine there is a locked safe where we store our most private, confidential, and secure information, data, and files. Yet, the key is not in our own pocket. The safe is opened by someone we do not know for us whenever we need it. Than the data transfer is accomplished for us. The safe is closed and locked again. This process continues over and over just like that. Do we consider this process safe? Well, we have to ask ourselves what changes when the process works digitally. When it is digital, the personal nature of the data does not disappear. Where is so much personal data stored? How is it stored? How is it secured? So how does it continue to be our personal and private data? Does it truly remain private after we share it?

The sad truth is that we do not know whether our personal data is kept in secret and secure. As individuals, we cannot do anything other than expect it to be. In that case, some international data security policies or legislation is still being developed. The General Data Protection Regulation (GDPR), data security policies and legislation developed in Europe, is the most visible joint action in the field of data security (Sharma, 2020; European Union Agency for Fundamental Rights and Council of Europe, 2018; Voigt, & von dem Bussche, 2017). Countries in continents such as Asia (Greenleaf, 2014), Africa (Makulilo, 2016), and America (Raul, 2019) also try to protect their citizens by making legal regulations in the context of data security policies. In Turkey, the steps taken in this regard are executed with the regulations made by the collaborative efforts of the government and NGOs (Kınıkoglu et al., 2019; Personal Data Protection Authority, 2016).

At the same time, due to the business models of institutions that become data-dependent, data technology gurus, futurists, and leading data science experts are signaling that they will invest every year in data security and encryption, crypto technology, etc. (*see* Gartner's Top Strategic Technology Trends for 2022). However, if personal data encryption and cryptosystems can be created as suggested by those who foresee this model, perhaps the possibility of living in a more efficient and organized world and society can be realized without the concern and risk of personal data security (Nyman, 2022; Nyman, 2021b; Deniz, 2021; *see also* Ejaz & Anpalagan, 2019). A little hope will not cost us anything!

However, the issue should not be overlooked just by considering it as an innovation. Let us say a technological development emerges that concerns the issue of data security. Today, this innovation on data has a certain place in the digitalized global culture. Companies use this innovation for their economic interests; states and governments are trying to use it for their "national interests" and "national security", etc. The truth is technology is advancing much faster than the process of creating laws in which general rules can be drawn up and adopted in a way that will have a binding effect as a set of regulations for the benefit of all people in a social consensus. In this context, if the technology is a supersonic jet, the enactment process of legal regulations has to advance at the speed of a steam train. Moreover, these regulations are often not compatible with the relativity of local laws that vary according to national or geographical boundaries. It is also seen that local regulations in a global network often turn from regulation to blocking and have no other result than causing unequal access to content for users in this network.

Users can obtain a visa to go out of their national borders in a virtual environment by connecting to the internet. As they began to disseminate the globalized data they obtained and the personal or local data they globalized, especially within communities, new rules began to emerge. Free from their partnership and belonging, no matter if it is country, state, geography, or continent, they can become a member of the social network they are in, provided that they accept an agreement called the "community rules" or "community guidelines" (*see* internetmatters.org., 2022), which includes some basic principles on how to behave in that community. Otherwise, they may not be included there or be excluded from the community temporarily or permanently when they act against those principles. That brings a new and more autonomous consensus on data security beyond the rules of state and supranational organizations, especially in online communities where users interact.

The set of rules that each company offers to users almost constitutes the set of rules that digital citizens or individuals have to comply with. Of course, it is not reliable to leave the guarantee of the confidentiality of this data to the relevant institutions or companies in various online data sharing areas, from socialization to commerce, from health to personal data used by governments and institutions in automation systems. Nonetheless, it appears that the concern that individuals will remain the most vulnerable to the risks to data security in this process will persist. In that case, the privacy of individuals interacting in an endless virtual environment open to data sharing is also an important point to be addressed.

Privacy in the Digital World

When the issue of privacy comes together with a concept related to digital, it will not be an exaggeration to think about the inevitable question: "Can there be privacy in a world where digital transformation takes place?" Therefore, an important issue to focus on privacy is not that someone can access our data without our knowledge, which we do not know in what form, where it is, and how it is used. Governments and companies have already owned this data for years to the extent that technology allows. Yes, laws and regulations are being made and will continue to be made as mentioned before. The issue is how effective and binding these regulations are for ensuring user data privacy, and most importantly, they are enforceable.

The fact that the institutional arrangements and the legal vacuum mentioned before, especially on social networks, are determined by the community rules creates a duality (*see the chapter:* "The Intersection of Privacy, Law, and Technology", Payton & Claypoole, 2014**).** In other words, while two individuals interact within the framework of laws and social and cultural norms in their real-life interactions, it may be possible for them to behave differently in a virtual environment such as on Facebook, Twitter, Instagram, WhatsApp, TikTok, and Snapchat, etc. You can even interact with people you do not have real friendships or any familiarity with in these environments, and you can express your feelings and thoughts boldly and recklessly "as you wish". This confirms the results of the research showing that most hate speech is produced on the internet and social networks **(**Tontodimamma et al., 2021; Matamoros-Fernández, & Farkas, 2021; Richardson-Self, 2021; Chetty & Alathur, 2018; Assimakopoulos et al., 2017**).** In this context, it is clear that privacy is not limited to institutions and companies obtaining user data or sharing user data on social networks.

In social networks with new and more flexible community rules, disturbing interferences that occur because of this "flexibility created by the virtual environment" in respecting the privacy of other users continue to be a problem. How much do we care about our privacy and others', for example, with our posts on social networks, the way we expose ourselves, our demeaning attitudes in expressing our thoughts, and showing off, consciously or unconsciously, that we do not hesitate to make? Do not we interfere with our own and others' privacy? While performing all these actions, we share our data and leave our behavioral patterns, attitudes, mentality, and characteristics to the data ocean. Of course, those interested in using them will not hesitate to acquire these data. Because today, companies continue to get richer by using people's private information in one way or another. Larger companies such as tech companies that control capitalism in the world today are already capturing this data. Others also buy this data from these big tech companies. Thus, thanks to the personal data and internet usage habits they acquire, companies learn the customer experience effortlessly and massively, and by directing and manipulating customer choices accordingly to market their products and services to a wider mass.

Today's most valuable commodity is personal data. In other words, all kinds of private information that turns into data. Therefore, privacy has become the most valuable asset of the digital age. Not only those who produce the technology but also the users contribute to it. That means we turn the wheel of this system together. Moreover, with this digital culture created together by companies and users, we continue to make free labor of these companies in the virtual space, where we exist more and more with our virtual selves. Thus, while sharing and revealing our privacy more, we continue to create and develop a new self. Namely, a virtual self conveys more existential importance for us in the virtual environment. For this reason, the real self continues to transform itself into a virtual in the digital space as an entity that contradicts the concerns about privacy and secrecy of personal data.

The Virtual Self

In the "Presentation of Self in Everyday Life", Erving Goffman examined the interactions of individuals in the daily life of an agricultural society in the Shetland Islands (Goffman, 1956). In his work, he demonstrated ingeniously how individuals present their selves and frame behavior in interaction. A new version of this kind of research that can be titled "Presentation of Virtual Self in Online Life" in today's digital transformation, perhaps will show us new codes, new norms, and new forms of social interaction. An interaction that is distinct from the face-to-face interaction of everyday life. Actually, in the last two decades, research on the use of and being on the internet and social media has been carried out under similar names (*see* Slater & Sanchez-Vives, 2014; Bullingham & Vasconcelos, 2013; Papacharissi, 2002). Still, more research on the virtual self in an almost completely digitalized everyday interaction era is needed to be understood comprehensively. In the period when the digital transformation is being completed, virtual self continues to adapt its existence to this transformation. That leads to the ongoing process that the essence of our existence will no longer be anything but our data in the future. It is not known whether this period will be a new era or expressed as such. Yet, it can be predicted that it will be an era beyond the stages expressed by the version numbers of the revolutions or generations that started in the recent past and are still on the agenda at the time of writing this chapter, in fields such as technology and industry.

According to some technology researchers and futurists, the Internet of Thoughts, or "human brain/cloud interface" (B/CI) technology, thanks to neuroscientists, will connect an unlimited cloud environment with each individual's own brain. A neural-nanorobotically empowered human B/CI might operate as a personalized conduit, providing humans with direct, quick access to practically every facet of human knowledge. Other possible applications include a wide range of alternatives for improving education, cognition, entertainment, travel, and other interactive experiences (Martins et al., 2019).

B/CI is a technology that will adapt the principle of the IoT technology in which all devices can be connected to the internet and the network autonomously, to the human brain. In other words, people will be able to access unlimited amounts and sizes of data with cloud access connected to nerve intersections and receptors in their brain, and not only that, but also they will be able to process this data. Thus, humans will turn into autonomous living organisms that can access the privileges only machines and servers have today. This will be a novelty far beyond the cyborg fantasy as intelligence embodied in cybernetic machines we have encountered in the recent past. They will be integrated into the digital environment more than ever before and will be functioning in harmony with it. If that happens, time will tell whether the existential reality of human beings and individual's already transformed virtual or digital selves will continue to exist as a meta-human or meta self. Nevertheless, we should consider the concerns about the existential mystery of posthumans. By aggressively overextending and thereby compromising the neurophysiology of consciousness, the posthuman situation may weaken human nature, defined as the effortless capability for transcending the mind's conceptual content (Haney, 2006).

B/CI is a development that can be the subject of many dystopian fantasies even on its own. Imagine that it becomes possible for a mind to have the opportunity to have or access all the knowledge of humanity. That would be a very exciting and very scaring innovation at the same time. Presumably, access to all that data would not have been granted equally to all humanity. In the end, what effect would it have on humanity, the existence of human beings, and the human self? If these researches leave behind a futuristic fantasy level and produce real results, the question of what kind of physical, mental, and most importantly existential effects it will have on people will probably be limited to answering today through predictions or speculations. However, in the not too distant future, we can predict that these topics will be pursued in-depth and more science-based than fantasy. Likewise, at the time of this writing, a new phenomenon - related to the virtual self - already surrounded the world, introducing the concept of Meta Universe about virtual reality in the digital environment. Metaverse.

Metaverse and Meta-Self

Before the Metaverse came into people's lives as a new concept, we had begun to see similar stories in the science fiction fantasies of recent years. The stories in the *Black Mirror* series in which the individual has gone beyond being a virtual self and almost completely transformed into a meta-self, have attracted great attention from the researchers studying the fields of art, technology, and communication. However, after Facebook, which is a large user network in the virtual environment, changed its corporate name to "Meta" and the company's CEO, Mark Zuckerberg announced that he would bring "Metaverse" as an innovation, the concept of a meta-universe has made a massive impact all over the World.

Meta is a word and prefix used to emphasize the subsequent word's concept, scope, or meaning as altered, transformed, or beyond how it was before. The concept of the Metaverse includes virtual reality and augmented reality combined with virtual selves or meta selves in a complex digital environment. Thus, what the Metaverse offers is a digitally transformed environment, that is beyond the offline real world. It is a transcendental reality of worldly entities. After the Metaverse, the distinction between virtual and non-virtual reality will come to an end or will shift to a different perspective, so the reality of the Metaverse will gain meaning and value as a reality on its own.

The word "Metaverse" was mentioned for the first time in Neal Stephenson's fantasy science fiction novel Snow Crash, published in 1992. The following citation depicts some features of Stephenson's environment of the Metaverse (Stephenson, 1992):

> "So Hiro's not actually here at all. He's in a computer-generated universe that his computer is drawing onto his goggles and pumping into his earphones. In the lingo, this imaginary place is known as the Metaverse. Hiro spends a lot of time in the Metaverse. It beats the shit out of the U-Stor-It. Hiro is approaching the Street. It is the Broadway, the Champs Elysees of the Metaverse. It is the brilliantly lit boulevard that can be seen, miniaturized and backward, reflected in the lenses of his goggles...It does not like any place in Reality, the Street is subject to development. Developers can build their own small streets feeding off of the main one. They can build buildings, parks, signs, as well as things that do not exist in Reality, such as vast hovering overhead light shows, special neighborhoods where the rules of three-dimensional spacetime are ignored, and free-combat zones where people can go to hunt and kill each other. The only difference is that since the Street does not really exist -- it's just a computer-graphics protocol written down on a piece of paper somewhere -- none of these things is being physically built. They are,

rather, pieces of software, made available to the public over the worldwide fiber-optics network."

Besides the Black Mirror series, we have watched fictional stories such as Ready Player One (2018), adapted from Ernest Cline's fantastic science fiction novel of the same name (Cline, 2011), filmed by Steven Spielberg who is also the director of A.I. Artificial Intelligence (2001). Netflix series Altered Carbon (2002) which was adapted from Richard K. Morgan's cyberpunk novel of the same name is another example. We can accept those fictions as some of the most prominent examples of stories that present a meta-universe, set in virtual space.

As technology advances and futuristic ideas and fiction about Artificial Intelligence develop, ideas about robots that look like humans or replace humans were being put forward. It was even suggested that these robots would have human-like emotions. Today, although humans do not turn into robots, the technology that will enable them to reach probably a meta-human that is attained or equipped with mechanical and memory functions of a new kind of entity will come soon. It is possible to see that examples of a concept that was futuristic in the past, such as the cybernetic and organism (cyborg), are used very effectively, especially in the field of the health industry, with mechanical transformations and modifications (*see* Miah&Rich, 2008**).** It will not be limited to science fiction narratives that the context of the integration of the human brain with the virtual environment or equipped with high cognitive or perceptual abilities. Presumably, the Metaverse will be the way the universe is experienced, which has been transformed into a kind of narrative form at a post-interactive stage, and the meta-human will be the subject of "Digital Storyliving" which would be the Metaverse version of today's digital storytelling.

So, after the introductory information above, what is the Metaverse? Metaverse is defined by Ball (2022) as "a massively scaled and interoperable network of realtime rendered 3D virtual worlds that can be experienced synchronously and persistently by an effectively unlimited number of users with an individual sense of presence, and with continuity of data, such as identity, history, entitlements, objects, communications, and payments." This is a definition that also has the general inclusiveness of the cyber Meta-Reality defined as "the infinite multiverse of realities that can be experienced, inhabited, created, and shared by humans" (Sipper, 2022, p. 1).

The Metaverse can be summarized as another dimension of maintaining worldly social, and cultural practices, and finances in a virtual environment. In this meta-universe, you will be able to exist with your own virtual version of your avatar, where you will have the opportunity to create an identity and self. By purchasing the products, you buy in the real world in this virtual universe, you will feed your avatar, dress it, give it a house, land, vehicle, etc. You can buy movable properties and real estate. Therefore, you will be able to build a new life in the meta-universe. It is already being discussed about some cities such as Dubai, Singapore, Seoul, and Shanghai that will be converted into being present in the Metaverse by creating their digital twins (Cohen, 2022).

- So, what kind of change will the meta-universe bring?
- What difference will it make in daily life practice integrated with today's virtual environment?
- What will be the social, cultural, and economic effects of it?

First of all, virtual reality will continue to take the place of everyday life's practices more and more. Of course, what this means is not just what the VR glasses show us. The individual integrated with this virtual life, we already had foresight about what kind of environment would be with games such as The Sims, which was a phenomenon, and Second Life, inspired by the novel "Snow Crash" released in the early 2000s. It will be a digital environment where ordinary people can do what they do in the real world with their avatars in the virtual environment, that is, their virtual selves. Whether it is a game or a virtual manifestation of reality, to exist there, you still need to work, fulfill specific tasks or look for ways to make a living with a worldly expression. To provide it, you must first obtain the crypto coins required to maintain your existence in the virtual universe.

The crypto money technology has become widespread in recent years both extensively in the digital environment and as an alternative to investment instruments that investors use in traditional finance and money market transactions (*see* Chuen, 2015). Over time, many institutions like commercial companies, IT giants, and sports clubs entered the cryptocurrency exchange by creating their crypto coins. As we know, cryptocurrencies have been in use for over a decade. A development that has been frequently associated with crypto coin lately is blockchain technology.

Blockchain technology is a kind of data storage and security system that can be defined as databases that store information electronically in a digital environment. Therefore, blockchain technology has a crucial place for cryptocurrency. Blockchain ensures users guarantee the security of the data record. Thus, it completes a trusted data process without the need for any other trusted third party. The primary distinction between a traditional database and a blockchain is how data is structured (Hayes, 2022). A database typically organizes its data into tables, but a blockchain, as the term suggests, organizes its data into chunks (blocks) that are linked together.

Today, most databases are centralized. A single record is maintained in a digital repository managed by a single business that records the information. What is important is that these digital documents are held and owned by a single legal entity. This paradigm is used for almost all digital and virtual information, not just bank data. Blockchain records are not stored in one place and are not managed by a single party or, in many cases, an identifiable group of individuals or businesses, unlike a centralized database. Rather, a blockchain "ledger" is maintained by agreement on a global network of autonomous computers (Ball, 2022).

The concept of the non-fungible token (NFT) has also started to be heard widely, just before the Metaverse. NFT is a form of the nontransferable and unique data unit that is maintained on a blockchain, which is a type of digital ledger used to keep transactions. Based on a digital ledger kept by the NFT, NFTs give evidence of ownership. Non-fungible tokens differ from other cryptocurrencies that use blockchain technology, such as Bitcoin, in that they are not interchangeable. Non-fungible tokens are digital assets that exist on a blockchain and can thus be distinguished from others by having unique identification codes and information. They cannot be exchanged or switched at face value, unlike other cryptocurrencies. Each NFT is irreplaceable and unique, forcing NFTs to break the cryptographic norm and making it nearly impossible to confuse an NFT and a fungible token (Clemens, 2022).

Metaverses offer an open and fair economy, aided by the blockchain's immutability and transparency. Furthermore, prices are decided by the fundamental rule of supply and demand, which is based on scarcity, as well as the on-chain value of an NFT based on its application, avoiding the possibility of pumps and artificial value inflation. Anyone in the Metaverse may create, purchase, and view NFTs in order to acquire virtual land, join social networks, create virtual identities, and play games, among other things. With corporations and people alike able to connect to Metaverse frameworks, this varied variety of use cases opens up various opportunities for monetizing real-world and digital assets (Stock, 2022). In other words, digital works can now have encryption that is originally registered. Thus, the original and unique copy of a digital product will be registered in the name of its creator or owner with this process, even if it can be digitally copied later. While performing these transactions, the crypto coin is used. That is to say, these digital products or their digitized and virtually transformed version are bought and sold by crypto coins, and their prices are valued in cryptocurrency.

NFT technology and Metaverse came to the fore in the same period and it seems that they will remain an important element of the virtual universe in the future. Before cryptocurrency, especially in multiplayer online games, it was possible to buy and sell the game character, avatar, pet of this character, or various tools, equipment, and weapons that this character had or needed. There were players and player servers that made a lot of money from this business. The digital game economy adopted in the Metaverse will continue to become expanding with the possibilities of blockchain, NFT, and cryptocurrency technologies to bring (*see* Davis, 2021; Russel, 2021).

In the Metaverse era, from an avatar we create for ourselves to buying a house and land in cities that will take place in the meta-universe, the original and unique product will be licensed to its owner with NFT. This development will lead to the spread of a new ownership and organization model for the virtual environment. Of course, this ownership also has a material value that can be exchanged in the real world's money in cryptocurrency markets. In other words, it will be possible to sell your product in the meta-universe and exchange your products and investments, varying from digital art to real estate from crypto money to real money or investment instruments. It is a cue that global trade will move to a different dimension soon.

Although we have some strong predictions about what the Metaverse is, the fuzzy areas still remain. What exactly its virtual environment will be, what its social and cultural effects will be on people, and what dimensions the real world will be affected economically by it, perhaps will become clearer in the coming years. Today, we are still talking about individuals who can build a virtual self in the virtual environment and attain a social and cultural identity with a set of digital-specific values, thanks to the possibilities of web 2.0.

However, the virtual world that will be created by the new technological conditions differs from the concept of web 3.0, which is based on the 'semantic web' definition that was expected to come after web 2.0. It is seen that the Web3 concept which is the decentralized internet and mostly based on blockchains, has been brought to the forefront by crypto money geeks and technology experts since 2020 (*see* Davis, 2021; Gonzales, 2021; Stock, 2022). Unlike the current web 2.0 phase, in which big tech companies owned platforms and apps as centralized entities, Web3 is expected to become a new and important phase in the evolution of the internet based on openness, decentralization, and greater utilization for individual users in the era of crypto-currency, NFT, and Metaverse.

Individuals can continue to exist in the meta-universe as these developments progress by gaining more control over their own data. It is not impossible. Of course, no matter where technology advances, we must not lose sight of the capitalist economic sys-tem's nature that centralizes anything while globalizing them. On the other hand, maybe everything will be going into a dysto-pian state in the Metaverse each individual will be completely disconnected from all the truths of the real world and work to keep their virtual self alive in a virtual universe. Who knows, maybe there will be no such thing as personal data security, free choice, or privacy in the future (*see* Black Mirror: Fifteen Million Rights). Still, one should not be pessimistic.

CONCLUSION

The Metaverse phenomenon should not be considered inde-pendently of personal data security and privacy issues. Techno-logical innovations have effects that will change and transform the vital forms of organization of the masses. Therefore, it is nec-essary to evaluate the social and cultural effects and economic consequences of this innovation, regardless of whether it is global, local, or glocal. While the group that has easier access to technology and is more likely to use or adapt to these systems as generations such as Gen Zs or Gen Alphas are more the subject of discussion about such innovations, what about the others? What about those who as a generation have already missed the technology train? Individuals, who have no access to technology? People who do not have the Internet and devices that can access it? While the World's one part is talking about technology concepts such as cryptocurrencies, blockchain, NFT, artificial intelligence, Metaverse, and so on, what about the other side of the coin? What about everlasting exploitation of the labor force, children living in war zones or lacking basic education, geographies where poverty prevails, and people have to grow up being exposed to hunger, famine, epidemics, and obliged migration? Could the unequal order of the world be eliminated by the virtual prosperity that new coming technologies will bring? Time will reveal the answers.

The whole issue is the aspects of the value created by technology, whether the environment is virtual or real, that directly corresponds to the existential and vital demands and needs of individuals. As long as human existence continues on planet earth biologically, would there be a life of better quality, equal and fair access to necessities for the great mass who cannot get enough today? Along the short remaining livable existence of the planet on which humanity keeps surviving, this must be the question to be answered. Otherwise, the day will come when a small minority, who will continue to consume the resources of the World in the real, natural, or meta-environment, will not be able to suffice the "commodities" of the meta-universe. When that day comes, this small minority will probably have a new planet where they can go and continue to live thanks to the opportunities brought by space technology on that day. So, what about the others?

Depending on the type of world we want to live in, the effects of technology will vary on humans' social, cultural and economic conditions. The decision will be made by humanity, whether they are meta-human or not.

REFERENCES

Assimakopoulos, S., Baider, F.H. & Millar, S. (2017). *Online hate speech in the European Union: A Discourse-Analytic Perspective.* Cham, Switzerland: Springer International Publishing AG.

Bal, E. (2021). Dijital kapitalizm çağında büyük veri ikilemi: Korelasyon ve nedensellik. In: Çokluk, N. (eds.) *Bilgi Çağında Siyaset: Büyük Veri Ve Siyasal İletişim.* pp. 351-362. Ankara: Nobel Bilimsel Eserler.

Ball, M. (2022) *The metaverse: And how it will revolutionize everything.* New York: Liveright Publishing Corporation.

Berry, I. (2021). Top 10 countries with the most data centres. *Data Centre Magazine.* https://datacentremagazine.com/top10/top-10-countries-most-data-centres.

Bullingham, L. & Vasconcelos, A.C. (2013). 'The presentation of self in the online world': Goffman and the study of online identities. *Journal of Information Science,* 39 (1), 101–112. https://doi.org/10.1177/0165551512470051

Cable Data, (2014). Telecommunications cables. *International Cable Protection Committee.* https://www.iscpc.org/information/cable-data/

Cao, L. (2017). Data science: A comprehensive overview. *ACM Computing Surveys.* Volume 50(3), 1–42. https://doi.org/10.1145/3076253

Chetty, N. & Alathur, S. (2018). Hate speech review in the context of online social networks. *Aggression And Violent Behavior.* 40, 108-118.

Christian, A. (2020). Turns out dumping data centres in the ocean could be a good idea. Wired UK. https://www.wired.co.uk/article/data-centres-underwater-climate-crisis

Chun, W.H.K. (2021). *Discriminating data: Correlation, neighborhoods, and the new politics of Recognition.* Cambridge, Massachusetts: The MIT Press.

Chuen, D. L. K. (Ed.). (2015). *Handbook of digital currency: Bitcoin, innovation, financial instruments, and big data.* Academic Press.

Clemens, A. (2022). *Metaverse for beginners: A guide to help you learn about metaverse, virtual reality and investing in NFTs.* Independently published.

Cline, E. (2011). *Ready player one.* New York: Crown Publishers.

Cohen, B. (2022). The 4 metaverse cities to watch beyond 2022. *The Smart City Journal.* https://www.thesmartcityjournal.com/en/cities/the-4-metaverse-cities-to-watch-beyond-2022

Corea, F. (2019). *An introduction to data: Everything you need to know about AI, big data and data science.* Cham, Switzerland: Springer Nature Switzerland AG.

Das, S., Tripathy, D. & Raheja, J.L. (2019). *Real-Time BCI system design to control arduino based speed controllable robot using EEG.* Gateway East, Singapore: Springer Nature Singapore Pte Ltd.

Davis, W.J. (2021). *Metaverse explained for beginners A complete guide to investing in cryptocurrency, NFT, Blockchain, Digital Assets, web 3 & Future Technologies.* Independently Published.

Deniz, K. (2021). Davranışların interneti (IoB): Kamusal alanda dijitalleşen insan davranışı. In: Çokluk, N. (eds.) *Bilgi Çağında Siyaset: Büyük Veri Ve Siyasal İletişim.* pp. 295-308. Ankara: Nobel Bilimsel Eserler.

Donoho, D. (2017). 50 Years of data science. *Journal of Computational and Graphical Statistics,* 26(4), 745-766. https://doi.org/10.1080/10618600.2017.1384734

Dunbar, R.I.M. (1992). Neocortex size as a constraint on group size in primates. *Journal of Human Evolution.* 22(6), 469-493. https://doi.org/10.1016/0047-2484(92)90081-J

Ejaz, W. & Anpalagan, A. (2019). *Internet of things for smart cities: Technologies, big data and security.* Cham, Switzerland: Springer Nature Switzerland AG. https://doi.org/10.1007/978-3-319-95037-2

European Union Agency for fundamental rights and Council of Europe. (2018). *Handbook on European Data Protection Law, 2018 edition.* Luxembourg: Publications Office of the European Union.

Goffman, E. (1956). *The presentation of self in everyday life.* Monograph No. 2. Edinburgh: University of Edinburgh Social Sciences Research Centre.

Gonzales, D. (2021). *Metaverse investing: How NFTs, Web 3.0, virtual land, and virtual reality are going to change the world as we know it.* Independently Published.

Greenleaf, G. (2014). *Asian data privacy laws: Trade & Human Rights perspectives.* New York, NY: Oxford University Press.

Groombridge, D. (2022). Top strategic technology trends for 2022: 12 trends shaping the future of digital business. *Gartner.* https://www.gartner.com/en/information-technology/insights/top-technology-trends/top-technology-trends-ebook

Haney, W.S. (2006). *Cyberculture, cyborgs and science fiction consciousness and the posthuman.* New York, NY: Rodopi.

Haranas, M. (2020). Microsoft's underwater datacenter a success; Azure Ahead. *CRN.* https://www.crn.com/news/data-center/mcrosoft-s-underwater-data-center-a-success-azure-ahead.

Hayes, A. (2022). What is a blockchain? *Investopedia.* Retrieved from https://www.investopedia.com/terms/b/blockchain.asp

Kelleher, J.D. & Tierney, B. (2018). *Data science.* Cambridge, MA: The MIT Press.

Kınıkoğlu B., Zengin, S. and Akdere, K.C. (2019). Turkey, Pp. 360-372. In: Raul, A.C. (eds.) *The privacy, data protection and cybersecurity law review.* London: Law Business Research Ltd.

Makulilo, A.B. (2016). *African data privacy laws.* Cham, Switzerland: Springer International Publishing AG.

Marr, B. (2015). *Big data: Using smart big data, analytics and metrics to make better decisions and improve performance.* West Sussex, UK: John Wiley & Sons Ltd.

Martins. N.R.B., Angelica, A., Chakravarthy, K., Svidinenko, Y., Boehm, F.J., Opris, I., Lebedev, M.A., Swan, M., Garan, S.A., Rosenfeld, J.V., Hogg, T. & Freitas Jr, R.A. (2019). Human Brain/Cloud Interface. *Frontiers in neuroscience.* 13:112. https://doi.org/10.3389/fnins.2019.00112

Matamoros-Fernández, A. & Farkas, J. (2021). Racism, Hate Speech, and Social Media: A Systematic Review and Critique. *Television & new media.* 22(2), 205–224. https://doi.org/10.1177/1527476420982230

Miah, A. & Rich, E. (2008). *The medicalization of cyberspace.* New York, NY: Routledge.

Morgan, R.K. (2002). *Altered carbon.* Great Britain: Gollancz.

Nyman, G. (2022). *Internet of behaviors (IoB): With a human touch.* Independently Published.

Nyman, G. (2021a). Internet of behaviors (IoB) – A Clarification. *Gote Nyman's (gotepoem) Blog.* https://gotepoem.wordpress.com/2021/02/

Nyman, G. (2021b). Behavior computation: Internet of behaviors (IoB) and human AI. *Gote Nyman's (gotepoem) Blog.* https://gotepoem.wordpress.com/2021/01/15/behavior-computation-internet-of-behaviors-iob-and-human-centered-ai/

Nyman, G. (2020). *On the edge of human technology: An essay.* Independently Published.

Opris, I., Noga, B.R., Lebedev, M.A. & Casanova, M.F. (2021). Modern approaches to augmentation of brain function: Brain-computer interfaces. In: Opris, I., Lebedev, M.A. & Casanova, M.F. (eds.) *Modern Approaches to Augmentation of Brain Function: Brain-Computer Interfaces.* Pp. 57-89. Cham, Switzerland: Springer Nature Switzerland AG. https://doi.org/10.1007/978-3-030-54564-2_4

Papacharissi, Z. (2002). The presentation of self in virtual life: Characteristics of personal home pages. *Journalism and Mass Communication Quarterly.* 79(3), 683-660. https://doi.org/10.1177/107769900207900307

Payton, T., & Claypoole, T. (2014). *Privacy in the age of Big data: Recognizing threats, defending your rights, and protecting your family.* Rowman & Littlefield.

Personal Data Protection Authority. (2016) *Personal data protection law.* https://www.kvkk.gov.tr/Icerik/6649/Personal-Data-Protection-Law

Press, G. (2013). A very short history of data science. *Forbes.* https://www.forbes.com/stes/glpress/2013/05/28/a-very-short-hstory-of-data-scence/?sh=5be41c3555cf

Raul, A.C. (2019). *The privacy, data protection and cybersecurity law review.* London: Law Business Research Ltd.

Richardson-Self, L. (2021). *Hate speech against women online: Concepts and counter-measures.* Lanham, Maryland: Rowman & Littlefield.

Russel, J. (2021). *Metaverse for beginners: A complete guide on how to invest in the metaverse.* Independently published.

Sharma, S. (2020). *Data privacy and GDPR handbook.* Hoboken, New Jersey: John Wiley & Sons, Inc.

Sipper, J.A. (2022). *The cyber Meta-Reality: Beyond the metaverse.* Lanham, Maryland: Lexington Books.

Slater, M. & Sanchez-Vives, M.V. (2014). Transcending the self in immersive virtual reality. *Computer,* 47(7), 24-30. https://doi.org/10.1109/MC.2014.198.

Spataro, R., Xu, Y., Xu R., Mandalà, G., Allison B.Z., Ortner, R., Heilinger, A., La Bella, V. & Guger, C. (2022). How brain-computer interface technology may improve the diagnosis of the disorders of consciousness: A comparative study. *Frontiers in Neuroscience.* 16:959339. https://doi.org/10.3389/fnins.2022.959339

Sperling, E. (2009). Data centers in the desert. *Forbes.* Retrieved on 08 28, 2022 from https://www.forbes.com/2009/06/12/data-centers-desert-technology-co-network-data-centers.html?sh=4031b70577e2

Steers, S. (2022). Top 10 Underground data centres. *Data Centre Magazine.* https://datacentremagazne.com/data-centres/top-10-underground-data-centres.

Stephenson, N. (1992). *Snow crash,* New York: Spectra / Bantam.

Stock, B. (2022). *Metaverse: The #1 guide to conquer the blockchain world and invest in virtual lands, NFT (Crypto Art), altcoins and cryptocurrency + Best DeFi Projects.* Blockchain NFT Academy.

Submarine Cable Map 2020. (2020). *Telegeography.* https://submarine-cable-map-2020.telegeography.com/

Submarine Cables. (2022). *Telegeography.* https://www.submarine-cablemap.com/

Tontodimamma, A., Nissi, E., Sarra, A., Fontanella, L. (2021).Thirty years of research into hate speech: Topics of interest and their evolution. *Scientometrics,* 126. 157–179. https://doi.org/10.1007/s11192-020-03737-6

Understanding Community Guidelines. (2022). internetmatters.org. Retrieved from https://www.internetmatters.org/connecting-safely-online/advice-for-parents/tackling-the-hard-stuff-on-social-media-to-support-young-people/understanding-community-guidelines/

Vidal, C. (2022). Neurotechnologies under the eye of bioethics. *eNeuro.* 9(3) ENEURO.0072-22.2022; DOI: https://doi.org/10.1523/ENEURO.0072-22.2022

Voigt, P., von dem Bussche, A. (2017) *The EU General Data Protection Regulation (GDPR): a practical guide.* Cham, Switzerland: Springer International Publishing AG.

INFORMATION AND COMMUNICATION SECURITY GUIDE APPLICATION AND DATA SECURITY GOVERNANCE

Yenal ARSLAN[*]

INTRODUCTION

To the Digital Transformation Office (DDO) established with the Presidential Decree No. 1 published in the Official Gazette dated 10 July 2018 and numbered 30474 following duties was given.

- To prepare the public digital transformation roadmap.
- To develop cooperation between the public, private sector, universities and non-governmental organizations in order to create a digital transformation ecosystem and to encourage their participation in the design and delivery process of digital public services.
- To give an opinion to the Strategy and Budget Department regarding the investment project proposals prepared by public institutions and organizations in matters falling within its scope of duty, and to follow the developments related to the projects implemented and to guide them when necessary.
- Developing projects to increase information security and cyber security.

[*] PhD, Ankara Yıldırım Beyazit University, Software Engineering Department, yenalarslan@aybu.edu.tr

- Developing strategies for the effective use of big data and advanced analysis solutions in the public sector, leading the implementations and ensuring coordination.
- To lead and coordinate artificial intelligence applications in priority project areas in the public sector.
- Developing projects for the development of domestic and national digital technologies by increasing their use in the public and raising awareness in this context.
- To determine a strategy for public institutions and organizations to supply digital technology products and services in a cost-effective manner.

In this context, DDO has published the Presidential Circular No. 2019/12 on information and communication security measures and obliges public institutions and enterprises providing critical infrastructure services to implement certain security measures in order to ensure data security. Following the circular, the Information and Communication Security Guide was published on 10 July 2020, and the Information and Communication Security Audit Guide was published on 27 October 2021 for the audits to be carried out according to this guide. According to the guide, public institutions and businesses providing critical infrastructure services should comply with the guide until 27.07.2022. According to the current version of the guide, the first of the audits to be done every year should be completed by 31.12.2022. However, the guide did not envisage any sanctions for incomplete inspections and lack of compliance.

Concrete targets to be achieved as a result of its implementation have been determined in the guide.

1. Encouraging the use of domestic and national products.
2. Preventing repetitive studies and investments to be made in institutions and organizations that will implement the Guidelines.
3. The three-level grading of security measures and the application of minimum security measures in line with their security grades to asset groups.

4. Configuring the guide in a way to ensure traceability of details about security measures.
5. To take Security measures can be applied independently of product and technology.
6. Supervision of the implementation of security measures.
7. Grouping the security measures in such a way as to ensure their applicability independently of each other and ensuring the modularity of the guide.
8. Ensuring applicable by all institutions and organizations.
9. Ensuring the sustainability of the guideline by taking into account the needs, developing and changing conditions.
10. Ensuring format and content of the guide should be original.
11. The guide should address both the personnel who will implement the security measures and the auditors who will check whether these measures are applied.
12. Compliance of the content of the guide with the legislation and framework of information security and national / international standards.

The content of the guide; In line with the objectives and targets, national/international standards and guidelines, good practice examples and current legislation have been taken into account.

The content of the guide consists of 4 parts, which are specified below.

- Information and communication security application guide
- Security measures for asset groups
- Security measures for application and technology areas
- Hardening measures

The following deadlines are foreseen for the transition process.

- 6 months to define the analysis and implementation roadmap

- o Identifying Asset Groups
- o Determination of Asset Group Criticality
- o Current Situation and Gap analysis
- o Determination of the implementation roadmap
- 18 months to implement level 1 set of measures
- 21 months to implement the level 2 set of measures
- 24 months to implement the level 3 set of measures

Institutions must perform the audit at least once a year and it is primarily provided by the Internal Staff and Internal Audit Units. After than the results must be sent to DDO.

According to the Audit guide, the audit stages are given as follows.

1. Identify asset groups
2. Determine the criticality of assets
3. Perform current situation and gap analysis
4. Set the guide application roadmap
5. Take action according to the roadmap
6. Have an information and communication security audit in accordance with the guideline
7. Monitor and check the guide application roadmap
8. Manage changes in contacts, if any
9. Manage changes in asset groups

More than 600 measures, classified in 3 groups as security measures for asset groups, security measures for application and technology, and hardening measures, must be implemented within the periods specified below, according to the criticality level,

1. Level measures must be implemented until 27.01.2022
2. Level measures should be implemented until 27.04.2022
3. Level measures should be implemented until 27.07.2022

In the article, the technologies that should be used for compliance with the Information and Communication Security Measures guide, which was published on 10 July 2020, will be determined for public institutions and businesses providing critical infrastructure services. Governance regarding the application and data security measures that should be implemented in IT units in order to ensure permanent personal and corporate data security will be discussed.

Guidelines Implementation and Data Security Governance

The guide, which has been prepared quite comprehensively, has taken the ISO 27001 standard as an example. In addition, it has been observed that it has been added to some regulations such as the Personal Data Protection Law (KVKK), which is prepared similar to the GDPR regulation used by Europe.

The standard, which is almost the same as ISO 27001, should be considered as an Information Security Management System (ISMS). In a way, it can be said that ISO 27001 is added to KVKK. However, it is necessary to anchor ISMS to our corporate processes to ensure its sustainability. Of course, for this, it is necessary to determine a wide scope that includes units other than information technology unit such as purchasing and human resources processes, without limiting the scope only to information technology unit (Carvalho&Marquez, 2019).

Auditors will be able to use interview, review, security audit, penetration testing and source code analysis techniques in audits. However, it may be beneficial to evaluate and consider the following issues in studies and audits within the scope of the guide;

- Institution's mission, vision, field of activity and service catalog
- Institution's strategic plan, annual report, performance program and action plans
- Organizational structure of the institution and the place and responsibilities of the information technology unit in the organization
- Institution's external stakeholders (data received/given via physical or webservice /API) and their protocols

- Audit findings such as previous Internal Audit, Court of Accounts, ISO 27001
- Institutional Information Security Management Systems procedures and applications
- 2020-2023 National Cyber Security Strategy
- Communiqué on Procedures and Principles on Connecting to the KamuNet Network and Supervision of the KamuNet Network,
- KVKK Law No. 6698
- Law No. 5651 on Regulating Broadcasts on the Internet and Combating Crimes Committed Through These Broadcasts

In this part of article Application and Data Security section which is given guide section 3.2 examined.

Before implementing the measures for application and data security, 2 important studies must be completed. Inventory management and Service management.

Inventory Management

It is necessary to evaluate the inventory under the following 5 main headings.

- Information assets
- Human Resources
- Software assets
- Hardware assets
- Structures (Building, facility, site)

There are various problems in keeping software and hardware inventory especially in public institutions. There are inconsistencies and frequent disagreements between the units that perform property management, accounting management and information management. For instance, there is no practice union in keeping software inventory. This kind of things need attention.

Service Management

Service management means providing customer-oriented IT services that are determined with the business owner, formalized by agreements, and meet cost and performance targets. Institutions information technology units should know their services and what kind of value they transfer to their stakeholders via these services.

All IT assets of the organization should be identified. A catalog of services available to stakeholders should be prepared with the appropriate configuration of assets.

Within the scope of Application and Data Security, which is part 3.2 of the guide, there are 110 measures and audit titles under 11 sub-titles.

Sub-headings of Application and data security measures specified in Section 3.2:

- Authentication (13 measures)
- Session Management (5 measures)
- Authorization (4 measures)
- Security of Files and Resources (7 measures)
- Secure Installation and Configuration (11 measures)
- Secure Software Development (8 measures)
- Database and Records Management (22 measures)
- Error Handling and Log Management (6 measures)
- Communication Security (7 precautions)
- Preventing Malicious Transactions (17 measures)
- Security of External System Integrations (10 measures)

Almost all organizations try to provide their security with traditional methods such as antiviruses, firewalls, intrusion prevention systems (ips), but they either ignore or are not aware that 60% of vulnerabilities originate from inside (Zadelhoff, 2016). Some of the internal vulnerabilities are risks based on software offered by the organization. Being aware of this, expert attackers have started to focus on vulnerabilities based on the source codes of applications. On the other hand, security vulnerabilities are frequently seen in web applications because software developers do not know the secure software development culture (Rodríguez et al., 2020). With the increase of cyber attacks and their types, cyber security expenditures are expected to reach 1 trillion dollars by 2024 (InfoSec Newsflash, 2019).

In order to protect the data, it is necessary to start with the conventional protection tools available in the institutions and to isolate the institutions from the outside world. As we all know, this is traditionally done with a firewall and a web application firewall (WAF). The first thing to check is whether these systems are up-to-date and whether their policies are in place.

In the next step, we can actively use database firewalls. You should isolate your database from insider threats, we know that today a very important part of attacks originate from inside, consciously or unconsciously. Therefore, you should constantly monitor your software developers, system administrators and application service users in databases and follow their authorizations. It should periodically share it with the relevant units and ask for the reasons for queries and updates to be checked.

When transferring data to your test and development environments, critical data should not be transferred, and data masking is required in mandatory cases. However, important data should also be masked in the production environment. In data sharing, security should be reinforced by using hardware security modules (HSM) as well as software encryptions. Institutions should share data with stakeholders via protocols such as webservice / API and SFTP over a closed line such as KamuNET.

ISO/IEC 11179 standard used in the world has been translated into Turkish by the Turkish Standards Institute. translated, and published under the name of TS ISO/IEC 11179. Known as a data dictionary, this standard should be implemented within the institution. The data dictionary has an important place in both inter-institutional data transfer and in-house applications to avoid duplicate records and to present accurate information.

By using data classification systems, you should classify your data with labels defined in your institution (such as confidential, private, top secret, service specific). Not only databases and data warehouses, but also all data generated by your users on corporate computers, all data sources such as sent emails and file servers should be classified.

Data lost prevention systems (DLP) are a major system in terms of internal threats. It is possible to identify employees who view, print, send e-mails, upload to websites, or copy data that we define as critical, with the DLP system.

A secure software development culture should be established in organizations where software is developed within the institution. In addition, static and dynamic code analyzes should be completed before the applications developed and purchased arc put into production.

Data manipulation operations such as select, update, delete made by authorized users through applications should be recorded. Essentially, such manipulation queries made by users are recorded through database firewalls. On the other hand But, we must discuss queries made within the applications, these queries are made to databases with application service users, so database firewalls cannot see real people. If there is no automation in an institution to record the manipulations made by real users, each software must make its own log according to the log standard determined by the institution.

In accordance with the KVKK, a special central mechanism should be established for those who want to make themselves forgotten by getting a court decision or by using your administrative mechanisms. These requests received through petitions or corporate applications should be managed from a single center.

Patch is the name of the packages prepared by software, appliance or hardware manufacturer companies to update their software (including firmware, microcode or embedded systems in hardware) for performance, speed, technology, compatibility, strategy, cyber security purposes or errors.

In order to test the reliability of the established data security system, internal and external penetration tests should be performed at the frequency determined by the institution, and the vulnerabilities found should be eliminated quickly (Vural and Sağıroğlu, 2011).

In order to keep the personnel fit about information security, trainings and seminars should be organized at the frequency determined by the institution, and posters for awareness should be prepared.

The issues listed below should also be considered.

- The weekly and monthly course of data leaks and whether the cases are reported to relevant authorities such as the investigator, prosecutor's office and KVKK,
- Whether the data controllers are registered in accordance with the KVKK law and whether the requirements of the law are fulfilled,
- Compliance of applications and updates to Log standards,
- Whether the queries from software developers and system administrators in database firewall reports are based on any official request,
- Evaluation of internal cyber security breach notifications and data from external sources and determining whether the necessary action is taken, whether these notifications are reported to USOM (National Cyber Incident Response Center)
- Whether the necessary actions are taken regarding threats such as viruses and spyware on the user's computers,
- Whether the data is destroyed in accordance with the deletion and destruction policy, whether the information in the inventories that are taken out of the institution within the scope of maintenance and repair and contain data is deleted,
- Whether the protocols related to the data transmitted to the stakeholders via web services / APIs are up-to-date and whether the data provided is compatible with the protocol,
- Whether clean table rules are followed or not,

CONCLUSION

An information security management system should be established in order to sustainably comply with the guide, which recommends the use of domestic products at the maximum level to fulfill the measures. The effectiveness of the established information security management system is also an issue that needs to be measured. (Meral&Bülbül, 2022). In addition to the classical firewall, antivirus and intrusion prevention systems, the following systems must be present in the organization.

- Inventory Management Software (Inventory Management)
- Information Management System (ITSM)
- Data Classification
- Data Lost Prevention (DLP)
- Breach and Attack Simulation Software (Breach and Attack Simulation)
- Secure Software Development (Static and dynamic Code Analyzer)
- Vulnerability Management Software
- Database Firewall
- Privileged Account Management (PAM) and Privileged account and session management (PASM)
- Web Application Firewall
- SSL Inspection System
- API/XML Gateway
- Security Information and Event Management (SIEM)
- Network Security System (NAC)
- Patch Management
- Network and End-user Advanced Threat Protection System (Advanced Thread Protection, Sandbox)
- DDoS Protection System

In the literature, there are licensed applications as well as unlicensed open source or free equivalents (Kaya&Öztürk, 2017).

REFERENCES

Arslan, Y., "Kamuda bulut uygulamaları", Retrieved on 05 15, 2022 from https://ictmedia.com.tr/Author/Index/55/dr-yenal-arslan/676.

Carvalho, C., & Marques, E. (2019, June). Adapting ISO 27001 to a Public Institution. In *2019 14th Iberian Conference on Information Systems and Technologies (CISTI)* (pp. 1-6). IEEE.

Cumhurbaşkanlığı Dijital Dönüşüm Ofisi (2020). *Bilgi ve iletişim güvenliği rehberi*. Ankara.

InfoSec Newsflash (2019). Cyber security statistics for 2019. Retrieved on 05, 15, 2022 from *https://www.cyberdefensemagazine.com/cyber-security-statistics-for-2019/*.

İç Denetim Koordinasyon Kurulu (2013*). Kamu iç denetim rehberi*. Ankara.

Kaya, Ö. F., & Öztürk, E. (2017). Veri ve ağ güvenliği için uygulama ve analiz çalışmaları. *İstanbul Ticaret Üniversitesi Fen Bilimleri Dergisi*, 16(31), 85-102.

Rodríguez, G. E., Torres, J. G., Flores, P., & Benavides, D. E. (2020). Cross-site scripting (XSS) attacks and mitigation: A survey. *Computer Networks, 166*, 106960.

Meral, S., & Bülbül, H. İ. (2022). Kamu kurumlarının bilgi güvenliği politikalarının kurumsal bilgi güvenliğinin sağlanması açısından etkinliğinin analiz edilmesi. *Gazi University Journal of Science Part C: Design and Technology, 10*(2), 314-329.

Vural, Y., & Sağıroğlu, Ş. (2011). Kurumsal bilgi güvenliğinde güvenlik testleri ve öneriler. *Gazi Üniversitesi Mühendislik Mimarlık Fakültesi Dergisi, 26*(1).

van Zadelhoff, M. (2016). The biggest cybersecurity threats are inside your company. *Harvard Business Review, 19*.

DATA SECURITY IN THE TIMES
OF DIGITAL CAPITALISM

*Zeynep Ekin BAL**

INTRODUCTION

Capitalism, as Fuchs and Chandler (2019, p. 16) put it, is the synthesis of several dynamically and historically evolving capitalisms. Financial capitalism, mobility capitalism, hyper-industrial capitalism, digital capitalism, and other forms of capitalism combine to form a dialectical capitalist unity of interconnected, contradictory moments. This situation can be observed when we look at the development process of the industry in the world. The First Industrial Revolution began with the mechanization that developed with the widespread use of steam energy. Then came the Second Industrial Revolution, also called the Technology Revolution, which even went farther beyond the social and economic transformation created by a mechanized industrial form that replaced the manual production before it. This age enabled humanity to enter an era in which people, commodities, and data were transferable faster by the railway network, telegraph, and electricity. That has paved the way for a transformation that will have profound effects at the social, cultural, and economic levels. The Digital Revolution, which started as the Third Industrial Revolution, came to the fore as the digital transformation and information age with the socioeconomic and cultural change, and transformation it created at the global level, which gained mo-

* PhD Ress. Asst., Istanbul University, Faculty of Communication, Radio, Television and Cinema Department, zeynepekinbal@gmail.com

mentum far beyond its precursors. The fact that the reflections of this became more or less decisive all over the world with digital growth laid the groundwork for the development of new technological paradigms. The importance and value of the data became a concept that has found its place in the digital world with its different dimensions in last two decades. We have reached the age of the Fourth Industrial Revolution or Industry 4.0, which is the time when machines communicate with each other, make their own decisions, and find their own solutions without the need for humans' constant control anymore.

However, digital data and the questioning about it, which started before Industry 4.0, continue to be a matter of discussion today. Scientific fields such as mathematics, statistics, information technology, and computer engineering enabled the development of some fundamental work areas and professions under the umbrella of 'data science' which are known today as data scientist, database administrator (DBA), data analyst, data researcher, data engineer, big data architecture, data warehouse engineering, etc. (*see,* Baesens, 2014, p. 6-7.; Chatterjee, 2022; EMC, 2015, p. 27; Hiter, 2022; Rane, 2021). Data science is a complex novel area requiring significant knowledge and abilities in statistics, computer science, data mining, mathematics, and computer programming. For this reason, data scientists are considered among the twenty-first century's leading experts (Schmarzo, 2016, p. 86). Technology companies' ability to acquire a massive amount of data from everywhere around the world and work on it has turned into a data collection phenomenon that affects all individuals who can be digitally monitored at a global level.

The relationship between automation, industries, professions, and nation-states shows the integration and expansion of digital technologies are at the center of a descriptive transformation of life, economy, and society (Neilson & Rossiter, 2019, p. 188). Thus, the data collection phenomenon is directly connected to sociocultural structure, political economy, and daily life practices of people. This inevitably led the concept of 'digital' and 'big data' to be among the questioning topics of social sciences and humanities. For this reason, the security and privacy of data stand before us as an issue that needs to be taken into consideration in a wide range, from financial transactions to daily social and cultural life practices of individuals.

When we approach the issue in this context, in the age of digital capitalism, it is necessary to ponder over the issues of data ownership and privacy, and security of personal data in a life cycle where surveillance in digital culture is so much integrated into the daily routines of individuals.

Digital Capitalism: The Political Economy of Data

Digital computing is now pervasive and influences many elements of modern life, including economics, governance, daily living, culture, education, welfare, and science. Fuchs and Chandler (2019, p. 2-4) reminds that, many researchers are concerned about the "digital shift" which is expected to fundamentally alter political possibilities by destroying old modernist dualities such as "subject/object, state/society, politics/economics, public/private, consumption/production, time/space, mind/body, labour/leisure, culture/nature, human/posthuman". This evolution has included cybernetics, automation technologies, mainframes, databases, artificial intelligence, personal computers, the World Wide Web, smartphones, geographic information systems, social media, targeted digital advertising, self-quantification, Big Data, analytics, Cloud computing, and the Internet of Things.

Technological developments have profoundly affected some of the essential dynamics of the world economy throughout the ages. The stages of the industrial revolution, which started with inventions that led to mass production and continued with digital transformation, artificial intelligence, and machine learning lately, carry on to grow the global capitalist economic system. Following the digital transformation, corporations based on information technologies have become some of the largest data companies in recent years. Some most known of them are IBM, Wipro, Amazon, EY, Google, Walmart, Numerator, Cloudera, Splunk, SPINS, JPMorgan Chase & Co., PwC, Alteryx, Civis Analytics, Sisense, Oracle, Looker, Teradata, and Accenture, just to name a few (*see* Marr, 2016; Duggal, 2022; Gottsegen, 2022; Kobylinski, 2022).

The world has become much more digitally transformed than ever before lately. Individuals and institutions continue to be stakeholders in this digitalization process every moment. As the data in the digital world increases and traditional small data processing methods cannot meet the need for storing, classifying, processing, and using this growing data, the 'Big Data' paradigm has inevitably entered the path of rapid development in the field of information technology. Big data has five basic features that are called the five V's of big data. These are *volume, velocity, variety, veracity*, and *value* (Hwang & Chen, 2017, p. 4). To manage such a high volume of data, considerable storage capacity and analytical skills are required. The variety indicates that data comes in several forms, which can be difficult and costly to manage effectively. The inability to handle massive data in real-time to extract useful information or knowledge is referred to as high velocity. The veracity suggests that data verification is tough. Big data's value differs according to its application environment.

Big data is stressed by Kaur and Bharti (2019, p. 4-6) as a general term that depicts the accumulation of data clusters that cannot be processed using traditional techniques. Different devices, systems, and structures are required to process extensive information. Immense information developments are mandatory to process the enormous volumes of organized and unstructured information in real-time to provide a more accurate analysis. That can lead to more remarkable operational benefits, price drops, and fewer dangers for business. *Operational big data* and *analytical big data* are two major categories in the industry. *Structured data*, which can be categorized and analyzed successfully, and *unstructured data*, which is a sort of information that cannot be isolated, turned into classifications, or quantitatively deconstructed, are the two basic categories of big data.

Big data has both pros and cons. There are several ways big data might benefit our lives, according to Zhang (2017), but there are also reasons to be concerned. The scope or lack of restrictions will be the topic of various discussions and political debates concerning big data. Whatever we do, our lives are becoming more exposed with each passing day, and we are being monitored more than ever before. Zhang optimistically argues that much of this data, mainly that acquired by the government, is utilized to enhance and secure our lives. Moreover, he adds that data collecting in the private sector is often voluntary, and it is up to governments to control its usage.

On the other hand, data not only concerns people connected to the internet today but also restructures the relationships between states, subjects, and citizens (Bigo et al., 2019, p. 3). That means data becomes a more social and political subject matter as its importance grows in the economic system. The economic transformation created by technology will become the basis of a social change process that affects different fields such as culture and value system, knowledge, and politics. Big data use in terms of political interests will become digital public opinion threatening (Morales & Córdoba-Hernández, 2019, p. 31-69). While people were positioned as audiences in mass media and user-consumers in new media before, they just became more data sources and producers in the age of big data today. With the usage habits obtained via data analysis, individuals become vital not only to buy more but also to be constantly present in the network and share in the continuity of the consumption-based cycle. In other words, people maintain this process continuously by creating new data or sharing and disseminating their and others' data online. To do this, staying on the network and giving their attention online is necessary.

As Shaffer (2019, p. 3-7) indicates, the supply and demand rules that historically applied to commodities (goods) and labor (services) now apply to information (data). That is the transition from an information economy to an attention economy, and the ramifications for how information is generated, shared and consumed on the internet. After moving from a period of information scarcity to an excess of information, information is no longer a sufficiently monetizable commodity to drive an economy. Because human attention is a monetizable commodity in short supply, content recommendation algorithms play a critical role in our information environment and economy. Today, one of the most precious assets for the capitalist system is not only the labor force but also the user data. Therefore, Big Data capitalism is a way of describing the latest developments in digital technology in the context of economy, politics, culture, ideology, domination and exploitation. (Fuchs & Chandler, 2019, p. 10).

This is exactly why technology giants are among the largest companies in the world. In the following years, the worldwide big data analytics market will increase at a compound annual growth rate of about 30%, with sales reaching 68 billion U.S. dollars by 2025, up from roughly 15 billion U.S. dollars in 2019 (Statista, 2022). The question is, whose data are those produced to make tech companies richer and bigger every day? The answer to this question lies under the giant corporations of digital capitalism. The problem should be considered about the ownership of the data or whatever is produced and shared on the internet-connected networks with those data.

Data Ownership and Privacy of Personal Data

Almost every device connected to the Internet and is producing many digital traces about interactions, operations, and movements, whether users are aware of it or not. What began as a seemingly liberated area has become the area where governments and companies began to collect, store, retrieve, analyze and present data that records what people do and say on the

Internet (Bigo et al., 2019, p. 3). One of the crises capitalism creates over and over is related to the ownership issue. Although the issue of the property has long been specific to products and properties, knowledge or information is today an issue that concerns property issues in digital capitalism.

In addition to questions about which data is made open, how it can be used and how they are employed, it should not be ignored the issue that such an opening supports the data ownership problem and data control of the capitalist economy (Neilson & Rossiter, 2019, p. 194). Whether that is a concrete commodity or data produced, it continues to be shared unequally. In terms of data, this inequality also includes persons' privacy. Thus, a crucial negative impact on the elimination of privacy is inequality in the privacy of individuals. Moya (2019, p. 248) defines the inequality of privacy as a difference between individuals in a society in which privacy is an amplifier of existing inequalities. However, contrary to other inequality, inequality in privacy is a distinction that pushes society to extreme ends.

Digitization has brought about a radical change in the field of data, as in many other fields. In recent years, digital data has become the most basic product required for the circulation of information on the Internet or in the virtual environment. The total quantity of data generated, recorded, copied, and consumed throughout the world is expected to increase, reaching 64.2 zettabytes by 2022. Global data generation is expected to exceed 180 zettabytes until 2025 (Statista, 2022). The rise was larger than predicted due to increased demand induced by the COVID-19 pandemic, as more individuals worked and learned from home and used home entertainment alternatives more often. Therefore, the volume of data generated and reproduced hit a new peak in 2020.

As the virtual environment continues to grow, processes and operations related to digital data continue to boost. This situation causes the proliferation of institutions and companies that use the data of both institutions and individuals. Thus, many institutions, especially those that carry out their commercial activities in the field of technology and informatics, have to improve themselves for the collection and processing of digital data. If not, they need some technology companies that analyze and provide the data for themselves to survive in the marketplace (*see* Gupta, 2022). Whether a social networking company or a company analyzing data from other organizations and sources it is, they have to work with an enormous amount of data. It is obvious that as the data shared increases, these companies are also growing, and new ones emerge in the marketplace. In January 2022, the top 5 countries in the world in terms of the number of data centers are listed as follows: United States: 2,751, Germany: 484, UK: 458, China: 447, and Canada: 324 (Statista, 2022; *see also* Hiter, 2022; Gottsegen, 2022). These institutions or companies often use their data with the permissions given by individuals when making a transaction on the Internet, installing an application, or joining a network. The data of individuals are collected through an agreement within the scope of data sharing and usage permissions or community rules that users have to give to perform or continue almost all their operations in the virtual environment. Nevertheless, it is also common to obtain users' data without their knowledge and pass it on to third institutions or companies.

Access to the information of citizens of different countries is not equal for states and institutions. However, in the case of digital data, the distinction between a citizen and a foreign is eliminated. Yet, in the data world, the agreement is expanded in a way that includes the difficulty of separating the foreign and contains all persons, the data citizen as a state supervision object (Guild, 2019, p. 282). Government requests for data held by the private sector have increased globally in recent years, owing to a number of circumstances. Governments across the world have long required business firms to divulge information about their consumers. This has resulted in an increase in government requests for what Rubinstein, Nojeim, and Lee (2017, p. 8) call "systematic access". They refer to "systematic access" as both direct government access to private-sector databases without the mediation or contact of an employee or agent of the organization holding the data, and also government access to vast amounts of private-sector data, whether or not mediated by a corporation.

However, companies, agencies, organizations, and authorities that produce many data about the various interactions of individuals have also challenged the sovereignty of data collection and production of states on issues such as population, soil, health, prosperity, and security (Bigo et al., 2019, p. 8). Although there are regulations or laws in some international organizations and countries regarding the collection and use of personal data (*see* Cortez, 2021; Fuster, 2014; Etzioni, 2015), it is, unfortunately, a mystery to what extent the data of individuals is obtained and used in a way that protects privacy principles.

Probably, there is no such privacy principle in a capitalist system that is organized to make anything consumable for raising capital. In digital capitalism, personal data are also sources of work done to increase capital. In other words, personal data is the raw material of digital capitalism. Any data system, Marz and Warren (2015, p. 11) argue, serves to answer questions about the information you have acquired in the past. When designing a large data system, the most possible problem is required to be answered. This is called "property rawness". The rawest data that is possible is tried to be stored. The more raw your data is, the more questions you can ask. Thus, the raw data of individuals serve as the raw materials needed to obtain more information. That shows digital capitalism exploits people's raw data as material. The raw data is then, turned into a commodity after being processed by tech companies.

As Papacharissi (2002, p. 20) states, the ongoing patterns of capitalist production can also commodify newly emerging technologies. These new technologies serve the commercial interests of companies, not the welfare of societies. New tools offered by new technologies cannot transform the economic structure on their own. As the dependence on the special interests created by the capitalist mode of production increases, democracy and equality are endangered. Thus, the commodification of resources related to the Internet threatens the hope of being independent and democratizing the environments revealed by this technology. For this reason, the ownership of the data passes to companies that obtain this data from the person, process it, sell it to others, take this processed data and use it for their own commercial interests, and these companies provide a free supply. In fact, when these companies use people's data without their knowledge, they are doing the same thing they did when they exploited a mine in derelict geography.

Moreover, while doing this, they exploit this labor by making the people who produce the data, work for free in various networks and apps so that they can create that data, share it online, and spread it. No one sells anything for free in capitalist economy. If you do not pay a product or service in the (digital) capitalist system, then you are (or your data is) the product. Beside the free labor exploitation, in Shaffer's (2019, p. 12) conceptualization; our 'attention' is the basic commodity of the economy of the digital world. The digital platforms we use daily are designed to manipulate and measure our attention. Since the platforms take their money out of advertising, they earn more money when more people spend more time on these platforms. An important example of designing platforms to create addiction is the 'attention economy'. These platforms are increasingly becoming news sources about mundane information for many people. Thus, the relaxed, passive addiction created by this platform is sufficient for users. This is a great danger for both individuals and society. Whether they are for socialization, entertaining, or to do their daily needs and routines in a range from e-commerce, and banking transactions to education and official tasks, they continue to provide the labor that meets the raw material needs of digital capitalism to produce commodities due to the data they create via the digital interaction they have.

Digital Culture, Surveillance and Data Security

As technology develops, the social, cultural, and economic changes and transformations it constructs progress in conjunction with each other. Digital transformation continues to show its presence in many areas of life, from business models of companies to daily socialization and cultural practices of individuals, and of course, in the area of surveillance. The nature of the internet as an inherently fluid surveillance space (Bauman & Lyon, 2013) tends to blur the boundaries that flow between presumed activities and categories. People not only encounter and experience online surveillance, but they also interact with it (Lyon, 2019, p. 65-66). Lyon states that surveillance capitalism is the source of the systems that enable many aspects of surveillance culture. He argues that much of what currently counts as a surveillance culture also supports surveillance capitalism.

Commodities and services are offered to customers using sales and marketing methods of digital technologies provide. Consumption products like various paid software and apps, in-app purchases, and games that are offered directly, and through the click-on ads that make profits from the users indirectly show the economic dimension of the digital culture, which is significantly developed in the digital capitalism age. In 2022, the number of ads an average person sees is between 4,000 and 10,000 every single day. Today's people, who continue their daily life practices in a way that is highly integrated with the digital technologies of which they are customers and users, constantly share their data in all their activities while they are online, inevitably. When we look at recent research, it is obvious that 2.5 quintillion bytes of data are being created every day in 2022 (*see* Wise, 2022). In an environment where such a large amount of data is created, the surveillance culture continues to dominate.

There are several ways to assess surveillance culture. Watching individuals in public and private locations using cameras and technologies that gather, store, transmit, and analyze data is a well-known example of surveillance in everyday life. However, there is a surveillance culture that individuals are becoming increasingly active as they use search engines or, more likely, social media in their digital interactions (Lyon, 2019, p. 69). In these digital interactions, many of our personal and sometimes very private data, which we do not know by whom, how, and for what purpose is used can be transferred to third parties or institutions. At this point, the risks of online interaction created by digital culture on data security also arise. User's personal data is not only obtained free of charge, but it is also possible to transfer this data insecurely, especially to companies. Thus, the third institutions and companies that obtain our data make various analyzes about those data and use them against us to sell their products and services more, thanks to the surveillance culture we engage in when we are online.

According to Lyon (2019, p. 68), the major dimensions of surveillance capitalism are, (a) multiple data sources are used, and everything is recorded; (b) data extraction operates as a one-way process devoid of connection or structural duties and reliant on "signals of subjectivity"; and (c) analytics implies that authority (spiritual) is being replaced by technique (material), resulting in "anticipatory compliance". In a world where digital culture is so widespread, it is hard to perform some needs with traditional and analog methods. When almost all the processes of institutions and governments are digitized, as individuals, we inevitably do many things in virtual environments by connecting to the internet. As Fuchs and Chandler (2019, p. 7) stresses, Big Data is used for generating new understandings of political, economic and everyday life through communication on Twitter, Facebook and other social media platforms. That is Big Data has changed human communication's actors, structures, systems, contents, effects, contexts, and power structures.

We should consider that, there were five billion internet users worldwide as of April 2022, accounting for 63 percent of the global population 4.65 billion, or more than 93 percent, of this total, were social media users (Statista, 2022; *also see* Wise, 2022).

According to the recent research Statista publishes, mobile internet usage is currently about 57 percent of the total online traffic globally, as internet users increasingly move to mobile devices to access the web. The use of instant messaging services, video streaming platforms, and social networking are among the most popular mobile internet activities. On average, internet users spend more than 140 minutes on social media every day, and Facebook remains the most popular social network globally. The internet has also transformed the practices of how items are bought and sold all over the world in the previous several decades. As more people purchase online, worldwide retail e-commerce revenues will approach 4.2 billion U.S. dollars in 2020. Mobile devices are handling an increasing amount of online transactions, making m-commerce a more profitable sector than ever before.

Whether we want it or not, we must accept how difficult it is for us to fulfill our daily life routines without adapting to digitalization. However, as we gain more digital literacy, we should become more concerned about online privacy, fraud, and hacking. In that case, the question of how can we maintain the conjunction of digital culture on individuals, which is not just social media or other interaction networks, without interfering with our private life or the security of our personal data is important. For this reason, the more we know about our data security as users and the more consciously we use the internet, the more we can prevent our data from being used without our knowledge.

While we remain a part of digital culture, we can think about strategies to protect our data security and privacy in the virtual environment. The following are some of the top things we can do to protect our privacy online (Aura, 2022; *see also* De Groot, 2022):

- We can share less online.
- We can use strong, unique passwords with two-factor authentication.

- We can tighten the privacy settings for your online accounts.
- We can clean unused mobile applications and browser extensions.
- We can prevent search engines from watching us.
- We can browse the internet with a safe VPN.
- We can make software updates on time.
- We can deactivate ads and data monitoring.
- We can use encryption to protect our data.
- We can cancel the unnecessary third party application links.

CONCLUSION

Marx analyzed capitalism and society as historical, based on a dialectic of continuity and change, and his personal method is no exception for today's digital capitalism, states Fuchs (2019, p. 54-57) and, claims that there are at least fourteen reasons why Marx is still relevant today. As long as capitalism and class prevail, his theory will be essential for comprehending, criticizing, and altering society.

People's daily life practices began to change more radically than ever before by the experience of digital transformation. Digitization continues to increase its presence in a wide range of areas, from the routines of individuals in their social and cultural life to the reorganization of the institutional working styles of establishments such as the states and companies. Digital capitalism, as a facet of global capitalism that is both the source and outcome of current technology breakthroughs, continues to encompass the entire world at an astonishing speed. More data is being created and exchanged than ever before during this period. Governments and companies use the data under a wide range of security and privacy risks, both on an institutional and individual scale.

While the states and companies have the opportunity and obligation to take various measures to secure their data, individuals interacting in the digital world are not always so secure in this regard. Because the institutions and organizations that already obtain the data they always organized, powerful, and much more unrestrained to use the opportunities offered by the inadequacy of the laws and regulations than the individual users are. For this reason, corporations' data collection of people issue is not only a privacy and security problem but also significantly parallels the class conflict that causes the capitalist economic system to exploit people's labor and provide unequal sharing. The class conflict of digital capitalism manifests itself as a conflict between the people who produce the data and the large companies that obtain and use it.

In the age of rapidly globalizing digital capitalism and big data, we should know our rights as individuals and societies to protect our data and privacy, and improve our digital literacy as more conscious digital users. As citizens, we should be more demanding from legislators and government to take more effective legal regulations and measures regarding our data security. As it should be in other social, cultural, and economic areas, if we seek our rights as citizens and strive to achieve them, then we can hope that our data remains more private and secure.

REFERENCES

Aura. (2022). How to protect your privacy online. *Aura.com.* https://www.aura.com/learn/how-to-protect-your-privacy-online.

Bauman, Z. & Lyon, D. (2013). *Liquid surveillance: A conversation.* Cambridge: Polity Press.

Baesens, B. (2014). *Analytics in a big data world: The essential guide to data science and its applications.* Hoboken, NJ: John Wiley & Sons, Inc.

Bigo, D., Isin, E., Ruppert, E. (2019). Data politics. In: Bigo, D., Isin, E., Ruppert, E. (eds.) *Data politics: Worlds, subjects, right* (p. 1-17). New York, NY: Routledge.

Chatterjee, M. (2022). Top 9 job roles in the world of data science for 2022. *Mygreatlearning.com.* https://www.mygreatlearning.com/blog/different-data-science-jobs-roles-industry/

Cortez, E.K. (2021). *Data protection around the world: Privacy laws in action.* The Hague, The Netherlands: Asser Press.

De Groot, J. (2022). 101 Data protection tips: How to keep your passwords, financial & personal information online safe in 2022. *Digitalguardian.com.*

https://digitalguardian.com/blog/101-data-protection-tips-how-keep-your-passwords-financial-personal-information-safe

Duggal, N. (2022). Top 5 data science companies to work for in 2022. *Simplilearn.com* https://www.simplilearn.com/top-data-science-companies-article

EMC, (2015). *Data science & big data analytics: discovering, analyzing, visualizing and presenting data*, EMC Education Services. Indianapolis, IN: John Wiley & Sons, Inc.

Etzioni, A. (2015). *Privacy in a cyber age, policy and practice*. Palgrave Macmillan: New York, NY.

Fuchs, C. (2019). Karl Marx in the age of big data capitalism. In: Chandler, D. and Fuchs, C. (eds.) Digital Objects, Digital Subjects: Interdisciplinary Perspectives on Capitalism, Labour and Politics in the Age of Big Data (p. 53–71). London: University of Westminster Press.

Fuchs, C. & Chandler, D. 2019. Introduction big data capitalism - politics, activism, and theory. In: Chandler, D. and Fuchs, C. (eds.) Digital Objects, Digital Subjects: Interdisciplinary Perspectives on Capitalism, Labour and Politics in the Age of Big Data (p. 1–20). London: University of Westminster Press.

Fuster, G. G. (2014). *The emergence of personal data protection as a fundamental right of The EU*. Cham, Switzerland: Springer.

Gottsegen, G. (2022). 35 data science companies you should know. *Builtin.com.* https://builtin.com/data-science/data-science-companies

Guild, E. (2019). Data rights: Claiming privacy rights through international institutions. In: Bigo, D., Isin, E., Ruppert, E. (eds.) *Data Politics: Worlds, Subjects, Right* (p. 267-284). New York, NY: Routledge.

Gupta, S. (2022). 22 best data science companies hiring in 2022. https://www.springboard.com/blog/data-science/companies-hiring-data-scientists/

Hiter, S. (2022). Top 50 companies hiring for data science roles. *Datamation.com.* https://www.datamation.com/careers/top-data-science-companies-hiring/

Hwang, K. & Chen, M. (2017). *Big-data analytics for cloud, iot and cognitive computing*, West Sussex, UK: John Wiley & Sons Ltd.

Kaur, K & Bharti, V. (2019). A survey on big data: Its challenges and solution from vendors, In: Mittal, M., Balas, V. E., Goyal L. M., Kumar, R. (eds.) *Big Data Processing Using Spark in Cloud* (p. 1-22). Singapore: Springer Nature Pte Ltd.

Kobylinski, S. (2022). The 10 most innovative companies in data science for 2022. *Fastcompany.com.* https://www.fastcompany.com/90724383/most-innovative-companies-data-science-2022

Lyon, D. (2019). Surveillance capitalism, surveillance culture and data politics. In: Bigo, D., Isin, E., Ruppert, E. (eds.) *Data Politics: Worlds, Subjects, Right.* (p. 64-77). New York, NY: Routledge.

Marr, B. (2016). *Big data in practice: How 45 successful companies used big data analytics to deliver extraordinary results*. West Sussex: John Wiley and Sons Ltd.

Marz, N. & Warren, J. (2015), *Big data principles and best practices of scalable real-time data systems*. Shelter Island, NY: Manning Publications.

Mayer-Schönberger, V. & Cukier K. (2013). *Big data: A revolution that will transform how we live, work, and think*. Boston, NY: Eamon Dolan Books.

Moya, B. (2019). *Data dictatorships: The arms race to hack humankind*.

Neilson, B. & Rossiter, B. (2019). Theses on automation and labour. In: Bigo, D., Isin, E., Ruppert, E. (eds.) *Data Politics: Worlds, Subjects, Right* (p.187-206). New York, NY: Routledge.

Papacharissi, Z. (2002). The virtual sphere: The internet as a public sphere. *New Media & Society*, 4, Pp. 9-27. http://dx.doi.org/10.1177/14614440222226244.

Rane, Z. (2021). 11 best companies to work for as a data scientist. *Stratascratch.com*. https://www.stratascratch.com/blog/11-best companies-to-work-for-as-a-data-scientist/

Robles-Morales, J. M. & Córdoba-Hernández, A. M. (2019). *Digital political participation, social networks and big data: disintermediation in the era of web 2.0*. Cham, Switzerland: Palgrave Macmillan.

Rubinstein, I. S., Gregory T. N., Lee, R. D. (2017). Systematic government access to private-sector data: A comparative analysis. In: Cate, F. H. and Dempsey, J. X. (eds.) *Bulk Collection: Systematic Government Access To Private-Sector Data*. Pp: 5-46. New York, NY: Oxford University Press.

Schmarzo, B. (2016). *Big data MBA: Driving business strategies with data science*. Indianapolis, IN: John Wiley & Sons, Inc.

Shaffer, K. (2019). *Data versus democracy: How big data algorithms shape opinions and alter the course of history*. Colorado, USA: Apress Media.

Statista, (2022a). Number of data centers worldwide 2022, by country. *Statista.com*. Retrieved from https://www.statista.com/statistics/1228433/data-centers-worldwide-by-country/

Statista, (2022b). Amount of data created, consumed, and stored 2010-2025. *Statista.com*. Retrieved from https://www.statista.com/statistics/871513/worldwide-data-created/

Statista, (2022c). Big data analytics market size worldwide in 2019 and 2025. *Statista.com*. Retrieved from https://www.statista.com/statistics/947745/worldwide-total-data-market-revenue/

Statista. (2022d). Global digital population as of April 2022. *Statista.com*. Retrieved from https://www.statista.com/statistics/617136/digital-population-worldwide/

Statista. (2022e). Internet usage worldwide - statistics & facts. *Statista.com*. Retrieved from https://www.statista.com/topics/1145/internet-usage-worldwide/#dossierKeyfigures

Wise, J. (2022a), How many people use the internet daily in 2022?. *Earthweb.com* Retrieved from https://earthweb.com/how-many-people-use-the-internet-daily/#How_and_Where_Are_People_Spending_Their_Time_on_The_Internet

Wise J. (2022b). How much data is created every day in 2022? [New Stats]. *Earth-web.com* Retrieved from https://earthweb.com/how-much-data-is-created-everyday/#:~:text=2.5%20quintil-lion%20bytes%20of%20data%20is%20cre-ated%20every%20day.,the%20growth%20of%20any%20organization

Wise J. (2022c). How much time does the average person spend on the internet?. *Earthweb.com.* Retrieved from https://earthweb.com/how-much-time-does-the-average-person-spend-on-the-internet/

Wise J. (2022d). How many people use the internet daily in 2022?. *Earthweb.com.*

Zhang, A. (2017). *Data Analytics: Practical guide to leveraging the power of algorithms, data science, data mining, statistics, big data, and predictive analysis to improve business, work, and life.* CreateSpace Independent Publishing Platform.

DATA SECURITY AWARENESS WITHIN THE SCOPE OF DIGITAL PUBLIC RELATIONS PRACTICES AND PRIVACY

*Mehmet KARANFİLOĞLU**

INTRODUCTION

Public relations (PR) practices vary in parallel with the developments in communication technologies and the progress of web 2.0 and 3.0 technologies and are increasingly acquiring a digital form. Such circumstances bring PR practices to digital platforms, which are currently digital public relations. The concept of digital public relations; effectuates the strategic relationship management goals based on favorable between the organization and its target audiences via digital platforms. Hence, conveying the PR career to the extended reality (XR) -most probably the metaverse- has evolved additionally. On the contrary, the digitalization of everything-things drives all business processes computer-based and refines them in data/info security.

Besides, it requires assessing the consequential data sources consisting of data pools on the axis of privacy. The information collected for PR applications, by all the information produced before, during, and after the application, must be stored and processed within cyber security measures. In this chapter, the subject is studied in-depth and contextualized, considering the information obtained from the literature and recent debates.

* Assist. Prof., Ibn Haldun University, Communication Faculty New Media and Communication Department, mehmet.karanfiloglu@ihu.edu.tr

The digitalization process started with the computer-based transformation of numerous known methods, defined as the digitization of information (Ersöz & Özmen, 2020, p. 172). In contrast, digitization is said to be converting analog processes into a digitized format by storing them in a computer environment (Karakaş, Rukancı, & Anameric, 2009). This form enabled the familiar analog processes of the past to be done utilizing computer software. It has resulted in computers and software being seen in many parts of life. The cumbersome structure of analog processes and digital forms has been affected by speed, variety, volume, and accuracy.

For this reason, organizations and sectors have started to use it. In particular, the global economy has become more centralized and widespread due to political and social events. The fact that far eastern countries such as China, India, and Japan gained strength against the developed economies of the past (Ersoy, 2017) in global trade and that human-based processes are increasingly seen as a powerful trump card against the declining population of developed countries has resulted in the importance of digitalization in the eyes of these triple economies. The concept of industry 4.0, named and designed at a fair held in Hannover, Germany, in 2011, has deepened digitalization (DeutscheMesse, 2014). For its part, with the COVID-19 pandemic that appeared in 2019 and impacted the entire world, the need for digitalization of sectors increased due to remote working and curfews.

Digitalization dramatically affects the characteristics of life, and due to the rapid development of technology, the world has had to cope with digitalization. Industries have likewise been a part of this transformation; by digitalization, the sectors have acquired the imperative software applications, transferred all the processes, from internal correspondence to the end-user, into the digital environment, and made the hardware materials compatible with the digital world. Senior management and subordinates had to make heroic efforts in the digital transformation process, which is imperative to promptly provide the necessary equipment and tools and provide the required information effectively. Nevertheless, it would be beneficial to focus on the issue of security by foreseeing the foreseeable problems that may arise from using these systems.

Albeit digital systems are practical implements in many ways, they are susceptible structures in terms of security because much critical information for the sectors is transferred through these systems and stored in them. According to data, by January 2022, 62.5 percent (4.95 billion people) of the eight billion human population are seen as individual internet users (Wearesocial, 2022). Even this data alone can inspire ideas about security issues, and most users of digital systems may not be aware of the risks and threats. Problems created by digital systems can result in economic loss for individuals, allow them to access the information they hold without permission, and cause irreparable damage by deleting or altering that information (Özenç, 2007).

Individual and non-individual factors threaten digital data security. Power, camera system, and switchboard failures due to natural disasters, email, internet banking, online shopping, hardware problems, computer viruses, and abuse of authorized access are just a few. As Wagner and Brooke (2007) stated, human-made threats are fundamental security problems, the weakest link in the chain that creates information security. These threats can appear because users use technology unknowingly or without proper training and deliberately damage the system (Tekerek, 2008). For instance, according to the Internet Security Threat Reports' data published by Symantec (2013) and Sophos (2021), cyber-attacks, spam attacks, phishing attacks, and virus attacks are increasing.

Amidst such threats, the PR profession and its practices are affected by becoming increasingly data-driven. In the PR sector of the world, big data is increasingly being adopted and trying to be the basis for best practices. Accessing, sharing, and using data requires planning. This study discusses data security considerations, which have been studied for years but are now receiving more attention in PR applications. At a time when the value of information is increasing, it becomes imperative for PR agencies to leverage secure online opportunities in professional practice without becoming a threat to providing specific data security.

Data Security in Cyber-Systems

The issue of data security can be addressed in the context of cyber security. Cybersecurity is a broad topic that includes the constant protection of the confidentiality and integrity of the information and data generated by individuals using the digitization process. The accessibility of data on the internet has made it necessary to take precautions with regard to the given security; therefore, this accessibility has led to crimes such as accessing, stealing, using, or destroying critical essential information from institutions. Data security focuses on the unauthorized performance of these behaviors, which can be considered a criminal offense (EntegreYazılım, 2018).

According to some news in *Hürriyet*, "F- Secure, one of the internet security providers Mikko, Chief Research Officer of Oyj Hypponen, claimed that the Fortune 500 companies with the largest revenues were hacked" ("500ŞirketHacklendi", 2015). As per the news, institutions become more vulnerable to cyber attacks as they transition into cyber environments. The topic of cyber security and data security will be able to present issues about vulnerabilities and threats. As individuals in the digitization process come online through their avatars on the system, their digital twins allow those who are available to survive virtual environments. However, staying in digital environments leads to the daily threat of hacking, data loss, phishing, or cyberbullying. As already existing problems have been observed, data security becomes even more vulnerable.

Conversely, cybersecurity agreements and legal sanctions have been prepared, and numerous cybersecurity system software are designed to protect data for individuals and companies. Smart factories will create cybersecurity software and systems by adopting cybersecurity measures for all their plans. There is firewall software that existing organizations are currently using. Although this situation offers partial protection, malicious software can be produced for up-to-date security software. For broader aspects, it raises issues such as cyber war, cyber threat, cybercrime, cyber extortion, cyber informatics, cyber sabotage, cyber espionage, and cyber-terrorism.

A review of studies undertaken looking at countries' attitudes on cyber security, software-related security vulnerabilities, leaked information, and cyber threats come to the fore. For example, they are finding a 10-year-old girl with a flaw in the Apple iPhone (Yeni Şafak, 2017), leaking the secret correspondence of countries with Wikileaks (Aydınlık, 2016), and announcing that the USA will consider cyber-attacks a cause of war (Milliyet, 2011), the emergence of the first cyber weapon named Stuxnet (Paksoy, 2012), the Anonymous organization's attack on the Telecommunications Communication Presidency -TIB (NTV, 2011).

Cyber attacks are carried out using two simple methods: DDoS (Distributed Denial of Service) and hacking. With the DDoS attacks, the country's internet system was rendered inoperable in the 2007 attack in Estonia. Sometimes it is carried out as a reactive protest movement: in 2010, DDoS attacks were organized against various ministry websites in Turkey to protest the ban on YouTube (Tufan, 2017). Several security systems have been developed in response: Router, Firewall, Intrusion Detection and Prevention Systems (IDS/IPS), Web Application Firewall (WAF), DDoS Prevention System, and Data Loss Prevention (DLP) (BGASecurity, 2013).

Another problem is that states are known to form hacking teams to fight cybersecurity threats and respond when necessary. Some cyber armies of volunteers and professionals, like the US and North Korea. Meanwhile, countries likewise have cyber security strategies: Canada, Estonia, Germany, the United Kingdom, and Australia. Cyber security will be one of the main areas of discussion. Smart factories, smart cities, innovative education, and other smart technologies that have entered or will enter personal life with digitization seem to facilitate most of the life process and concisely surround individuals. However, as with any innovative technology, these developments make the issue of security a bit trickier. For example, when surveillance cameras first came out, it was thought that they could effectively solve specific problems such as theft, homicide, and traffic accidents (Silva & Larsen, 2011). Now all crimes are solved by surveillance cameras. However, there are very few areas that do not have surveillance cameras at the level we have today. It brought discussion issues such as the privacy of private life and a panoptic social structure.

Being everywhere has also brought with it the ability to be observed anytime, anywhere. Every step has become traceable, whether in real life or the virtual environment. We discussed these benefits in the previous sections, Big Data Analytics, the Internet of Things, and New Ways to Communicate. However, all the technologies mentioned here still entail security problems.

Digitalization and The End of Privacy

Digitalization has become one of the most important developments of the last century and affects many areas. Experienced digital transformations affect companies, brands, and institutions as well as societies. There is a digitalization effect in many fields such as economy, politics, and education, and the only common point of the changes in these fields, which differ according to job status and industry, are digital transformations. All public institutions, private or official organizations that realize these transformations have become a branch of the digital world (Şahinaslan & Şahinaslan, 2018, p. 423). Digitalization directs companies to change and manage this change to the conditions of the age.

The concept of digitalization is affecting all sectors with its increasingly popular effect. In this respect, unique digitization methods can be found in every industry. In general, digitization refers to becoming computer-based. Because of this, many processes performed with computer hardware and software can be overlooked by digitization. Other concepts are proposed from this point of view: Industry 4.0. In Industry 4.0, many hardware and software transformations for the dehumanization of factories and artificial intelligence and autonomous robots to work with the dark factory model within the factory are expressed.

In this private space, which lies outside the social sphere, the individual freely decide where, when, and how to communicate with other people. Their criteria and value judgments govern the dominance of individuals in this area. This situation, i.e., the differentiation of the understanding of privacy from one individual to the next, further blurs the boundaries of privacy (Uğurlu, 2018, p. 258). *Privacy* is a concept brought to the fore by the reality of the individual, sociocultural, economic, and political developments, along with 19th-century enlightenment philosophy and modern understanding of science (Yılmaz, 2012, p. 249). In addition to philosophy and law, the concept of privacy has changed over time, society and culture. The idea of privacy has been, and continues to be, widely debated with individuals' widespread use of the internet and, primarily, social media. However, privacy debates are raging across generations because of their varying degrees of use of social media. Today, as the distinction between private and non-private has become increasingly uncertain, it has become more difficult for people to define their privacy boundaries. People who use social media intensively are not afraid to share topics, information, and images that many people consider private in these media.

Privacy is a fundamental human right. It forms the basis for rights such as freedom of association and freedom of expression that support human dignity. The concept of privacy is an essentially modern human right. Then again, privacy is one of the most challenging concepts to define of all human rights. Although definitions of privacy differ in many contexts, widespread reports of privacy in law focus on physical, regional, information and communications privacy. As a concept, privacy refers to a realm in which people can be alone, think, act, and decide what boundaries they set for relationships and communication with others (Yüksel, 2003, p. 182). In this context, the right to privacy can be understood as the right of individuals to determine the extent to which they share their living space with others.

The techniques and analysis that have emerged with big data applications show that traditional methods of protecting the privacy of individuals will no longer be effective. In this direction, many countries are developing laws and regulations regarding data protection and confidentiality. These privacy laws focus on individual consent and the collection of personal information. However, that is no longer enough these days. Because individual assistance in collecting personal information is provided during data collection, much of the information used in online procedures may contain important notices for individuals while not linked to personal information. At this point, personal data may be obtained, consistent with the interpretation of the data collected, through methods such as recording online behavior and keeping log records (Tan & Pivot, 2015, p. 860). This situation raises concerns about the protection of privacy. A closer examination of the literature reveals the privacy concerns of individuals. Several studies have examined the lack of knowledge about the subject, and the thought that individuals do not have control increase privacy concerns (Dinev & Hart, 2005; Dwyer, Hiltz, & Passerini, 2007; Goettke & Christiana, 2007; Miltgen, 2009; Ridley-Siegert, 2015; Tan & Pivot, 2015). The students are further analyzed in studies on the topic. In related research, while students' awareness of privacy concerns and Facebook usage is high, and they are aware of the potential consequences of sharing personal information, they feel comfortable enough to use personal information on these platforms (Govani & Pashley, 2014).

It is pretty surprising that online social networking studies challenge the common assumption that young people do not protect their confidential information. Research shows that young people employ various self-developed protective strategies in these environments. These strategies include using pseudonyms and providing false information, accessing personal profiles, setting privacy controls, limiting friend requests, and deleting tags and photos (Boyd & Hargittai, 2010; Miltgen & Peyrat-Guillard, 2014; Young & Quan-Haase, 2013).

The fact that data become personal data or represents a specific person can only be unavoidable during data processing. Processing of personal data includes processes such as collecting, recording, editing, adapting, transforming, using, explaining, combining, and deleting data (Kaya, 2011). According to the Organization for Economic Co-operation and Development (OECD), the principles to be considered in the protection and processing of personal data, published in 1980 and updated in 2013, are (2013):

- Irritability
- Quality
- Purpose Specificity
- Usage Limitation
- Security
- Openness
- Consent of the Individual
- Accountability

Although the protection of personal data is a topic that has been studied for a long time, with the rapid development of technology, the topic has started to be interpreted from different perspectives by changing its dimension. Personal data protection has gained international importance due to global data movements and traffic between countries (Akıncı, 2017, p. 2). In addition, efforts by countries to bring their legal infrastructures into line with technological developments have increased in recent years.

In the processes experienced, the existence of individual and societal defense mechanisms against threats to personal data gains in value. The protection of personal data is fundamental to the right to respect for private and family life. Personal data protection is interpreted in international documents with data protection regulations. Confidentiality, the confidentiality of private life, and international laws regarding personal data are monitored as follows:

First, we see that *Article 12* of the *United Nations Universal Declaration of Human Rights* was issued in 1949. *Article 17* of the *United Nations Covenant on Personal and Political Rights* was also regulated in 1966 as a right to privacy. The *OECD* published the text titled "*Guiding Principles on the Protection of Privacy and Transboundary Data Flow*" in 1980. The other is defined in *Article 8* of the *Council of Europe's European Convention on Human Rights* as the right to respect for private and family life. *The European Union Directive No. 95/46* on the protection of natural persons with regard to the processing of personal data and on the free movement of such data guarantees the same protection of personal data in every member country. Finally, the European Parliament passed the General Data Protection Regulation (GDPR) on April 14, 2016, (Eroğlu, 2018, p. 135).

In addition, there are some other regulations in Turkey, which can be summarized as follows: *Articles 20, 21* and *22* of the *Turkish Constitution* regulate the title of "*Privacy and Protection of Private Life*." *Article 24* of the "*Turkish Civil Code*" contains regulations regarding the right to privacy. The 21st Article of the "Acquisition of Information Law" regulates privacy-related matters. *Articles 10, 125, 134, 135, 136, 137* and *280* of the "*Turkish Penal Code*" contain privacy regulations. In 2016, the law study on the subject was completed. "*Personal Data Protection Law No. 6698*" was published in the Official Gazette dated 7 April 2016, numbered 29677 and entered into force (Eroğlu, 2018, p. 135).

Digital Public Relations Practices and Privacy

The view of PR as a profession aligns with the 1900s. Although the activities of Phineas Taylor Barnum previously formed the basis of public relations, it flourished in 1906, owing to Ivy Ledbetter Lee, a journalist, and advisor of John Davison Rockefeller (Tortop, 1993, p. 13-14). In 1916, he founded his first PR office, and in this agency, he used truthful communication as a public relations method. In this direction, the agency used "Accuracy, Authenticity and Interest" as its slogan (Turney, 2015).

Another critical name was Edwards Bernays in 1913. Bernays' most significant job was to increase public support for the United States Administration's entry into World War I (Şen, 2012, p. 67). Over time it has developed and changed professionally in PR. According to Grunig and Hunt (1984), public relations practices can be examined in four different models: Press agentry/publicity (1850-1900), public information (1900-1920), two-way asymmetrical communication (1920 and later), two-way symmetrical communication (the late 1960s and after 1970).

As in other areas, pacing with the latest technology world is also an essential topic in PR. The internet has enormous potential for PR and other communication disciplines and has become a strategic tool for PR departments. PR professionals can leverage the wired global village for instant, engaging, and persuasive communications. Generally speaking, while traditional public relations practices persist today, the internet brings new tools and conveniences to the public relations field. PR practices in the digital environment represent a communication opportunity (Petrovici, 2014, p. 80). In other words, *digital public relations* is the management of communication between an organization and its stakeholder, target group, target audience, and the public through internet applications. In addition, digital public relations is the state of the art of PR in digital media (Sönmez, 2020, p. 188).

The historical development of PR has significantly influenced the design of today's modern and digital approaches. Today, the Public Relations Association of America (PRSA) defines the term as a strategic communication process that builds mutually beneficial relationships between organizations and their public (PRSSA, 2022). Due to the digital transformation, technological developments have led to an increase and spread of production; Changing the balance between supply and demand in the opposite direction has played a role in the emergence of the latest information economy and the path leading to PR digital outreach. Digital transformation affects all sectors, including public relations. The increase in the value of information, the replacement of personal computers with smartphones, the shift to phone applications instead of programs, and the rise of new media platforms have all led to the emergence of digital data. Companies with intellectual and property rights to the new generation of digital products, where production has left technology and information to their own devices, have experienced a profound change in the entire business world (Ljungqvist & Wilhelm-Jr, 2003) that has led to the accumulation of data in heaps and the developments called Big Data.

The process of converting big data, confidential and raw data groups into helpful information and then analyzing it is done automatically with programs and techniques and offers benefits in many areas based on the authority the technology confers (Taşçı & Şamlı, 2020, p. 89). This data is growing, and much vital information for companies is embedded in the resulting mountains of data. The economic value of significant data increases when it is made meaningful with current processing techniques such as statistics, data mining, artificial intelligence, machine learning, and deep learning. Acting on this data has become a necessity for PR.

Thanks to this data, organizations; can identify the wants, needs and expectations of their target groups through research and produce different products, services and experiences of their competitors. While PR professionals listen to the wants and needs of audiences and individuals, their digital expectations must also be considered. Ultimately, it is crucial for organizations to meet these PR expectations on the road to reputation (Barnett, Jermier, & Lafferty, 2006). By reinforcing the perception that institutions provide value, corporate reputation has attracted various academic disciplines' attention and has increasingly become focused (Chun, 2005; Gotsi & Wilson, 2001).

The work and tasks of PR agencies and experts are increasing and diversifying with the new generation, digital applications, and business understandings. Nowadays, in PR there are activities aimed at informing the public about a company's products, services and activities, changing attitudes and behavior, raising awareness and creating selective perception, in addition to some basic company actions like the uphold the company's existence, corporate culture and philosophy. Implementation of printed, visual and digital activities to characterize and fulfill all types of activities, creating a trusted brand, proceeding with the marketing public relations activities and social media management in line with the expectations of target groups and stakeholders, in accordance with the company's goals, vision and mission are some of the recent PR assignments (Newsom, Turk & Kruckeberg, 2012).

Defining and maintaining processes based on the information and digital applications for *digital public relations* studies has become essential to PR processes. Individuals, who are the target audience of PR agencies and the companies they serve, are no longer passive in the communication established with them by the institutions; they are not only the crowd who receive the messages sent and act accordingly. They have become sources that follow all kinds of data and produce their data. With web 2.0 technology, individuals have become able to interact with institutions through smartphone applications, and institutions' reputations are built on sensitive ground, on much more diverse issues and individuals who may take immediate action.

At the same time, these people use digital communication channels to obtain more information about products and services than is provided. Additionally, the businesses that individuals may reach not only know what type of product or service they are responding to what needs; Based on the technical information, comparative comments, likes and complaints about the products, how well they satisfy other consumers and whether they engage in legal or unethical activities.

In the new digital universe, the fact that individuals can switch digital services and products very quickly means that they can easily switch from one product and service to another, adding new dimensions to the selection criteria for comparable products and services (Whitten & Leidner, 2006). This situation requires that institutions need more digital public relations practices. Due to the nature of PR, as the crowds change, there is a need for the use of new tools. Therefore, the earlier and faster institutions implement new communication technologies, the greater their competitive advantage (Özpınar, 2021).

Though, the digital transformation brings the amount of data produced to step values that cannot be expressed with numbers known at the standard level. Instead of numbers, the quantities are difficult to understand because of the zeros in them. According to the calculations, an average of 2.5 quintillion data is produced daily. Google processes more than twenty petabytes of data daily, and about 3.5 billion searches are performed. Currently, as of 2020, there are forty-four zettabytes of data (Vuleta, 2021).

Cyber-physical systems, autonomous robots, three dimensions (3D) printers, artificial intelligence, big data, the internet of things (IoT), wearable technologies, augmented virtual reality technologies, metaverse and other online platforms open the doors for new PR applications, and this leads to more data production and consumption. This large amount of data created and consumed has become too large to be managed with traditional internal data storage and processing systems, and requires specialized hardware, software, and processes to store and manage it. According to data from 2020, data production was more than 118.8 zettabytes, and it showed that users store this data at a rate of two percent. However, by 2025, the amount of data produced is expected to reach 180 zettabytes, and the data storage business is expected to grow by 19.2 percent (Petrov, 2022). These modern technologies listed above are fundamental for organizations, individuals, businesses, communities, and governments as they have started to be at the center of any digital transformation (Manyika, et al., 2011).

Both the regulations on the protection of personal data and the preferences of individuals, cyber security approaches, producing information from data, using big data in PR processes, "generating knowledge from big data is a demanding, complex process" (Wiencierz & Röttger, 2019) optimizing all these changes and requirements, and ensuring that it is ergonomic and usable for all stakeholders in the ecosystem is a challenging and complex process. Data from PR and corporate communication agencies, internal communication data and feedback from the company's communication channels, publicly shared data, and PR data derived from events and sponsorships.

This data can also be incorporated into many digital public relations applications. Additionally, user information, referred to as a digital footprint in digital public relations, may consist of content such as social media statistics that may directly concern PR specialists (Wright & Hinson, 2008). In addition to this data, there is data from the company's communication channels (first-party), competitors' marketing and advertising activities (second-party), and social media (third-party) (Weiner & Kochhar, 2016, p. 8). This data can be used to analyze audience behavior and preferences. Studies can be conducted to change user knowledge, attitudes, and behavior in digital public relations and to raise awareness of corporate social responsibility activities, crisis management, image management, reputation management, and social media management. This data can be used to develop digital PR strategies in the field. In general, the tools used in digital outreach are listed as follows (Tanyıldızı, 2021, p. 52-75):

- Wikis
- Blogs and corporate blogs
- Microblogs
- Forums
- Social bookmarks
- Podcasting
- Social networks:
  o Facebook
  o Twitter
  o Instagram
  o LinkedIn
  o YouTube
- Corporate websites

A strategic digital public relations application may be realized by disclosing the statistical data, correlations, or trends created from the traces left by the users in digital public relations studies (Stacks, 2016).

As can be seen, when PR is considered from the perspective of digital transformation, data emerges as the number one element. While performing digital transformation in an environment where such data is produced, data privacy and security have likewise become essential concepts. Regardless of the subject, users have become more conscious and sensitive about protecting their data in the digital environment. As with the actions conducted on social media, digital public relations applications try to collect data in the background. This data and its use; policy changes in the organization's strategy determination and activities are effective on significant financial results such as market share for organizations.

In 2021, the WhatsApp instant communication application operating under Meta (Formerly Facebook) announced that it would adjust the data processing policies, and its users reacted to this (Wijoyo, Limakrisna & Suryanti, 2021). Meanwhile, security-related problems and information leaks may leave institutions in a challenging situation. An example is a hacking attack that Apple experienced in the iCloud service in 2014 and the subsequent leaking of privileged information (Kovach, 2014). Data usage comparisons later with alternative applications revealed the importance of long-lasting differences in perspective and personal data security (Sindermann, Lachmann, Elhai & Montag, 2021).

With these processes, the concept of data governance is also evolving, which includes storing, protecting, viewing, using, modifying and processing data obtained only from the owner and authorized parties, and many studies have been conducted on the subject (Khatri & Brown, 2010). Based on these studies, the privacy issue is a critical topic of discussion.

The issue of data protection can be one of the topics of discussion in relation to digital public relations. Apart from unlimited storage of information using Internet technologies, the features of some applications violate users' privacy. The software developed is offered for use with backdoors so that future problems can be solved more easily. These backdoors not only interfere with the application but also allow users' movements within the application to be viewed (Öztekin & Öztekin, 2010, p. 536). While applications developed for free make everyday life easier for users, they create themselves a database with the information entered during registration and access to the content on the phone. Surveillance and privacy are two related phenomena. When privacy is violated, there must be an act of surveillance. Although data breaches have been critical in surveillance from ancient times to the present day, the structure of surveillance has changed in tandem with developments in business, information, and, most importantly, technology. This change has brought a different meaning and perspective to the violation of restricted areas. Today, the sense of surveillance and control has increased, and modern people have started to have less privacy (Langenderfer & Miyazaki, 2009, p. 381).

Sharing based on user claims in digital environments can allow data to spread unchecked. While making this data public makes it copyable or usable, it can simply pose serious legal problems. Individuals may knowingly or unknowingly collect personal information through digital platforms. A study conducted at the University of North Carolina found that 96.2% of teens disclosed their birthday, 83.2% their relationship status, 74.7% their political views, and 16.4% their cell phone number (Tüfekçi, 2008, p. 23). Although the data shared with other users may seem harmless, websites ask for information such as date of birth or mobile phone to change passwords; There are severe problems with virtual cheating. Individuals may face negative consequences related to cyberbullying as a result of this information.

CONCLUSION

The topic of data protection is becoming increasingly important alongside the topic of data security. Data protection is an issue that is particularly important for both individuals and institutions and must be taken seriously. Technological developments that are the result of Big Data and other digitization are leading to enormous increases in data production worldwide. It is about the security and protection of the storage, processing and evaluation of this data for various purposes related to data security.

As in other professions, PR has acquired a digital form in which the internet and its applications are used to get its share of digitization. The presence of the masses in the new media increases data production and enables the realization of digital applications in public relations. PR specialists will hardly have competent people to manage these applications via digital platforms. It is undeniable that in the future there will be a need for PR specialists who are experts in digital predisposition and data security. Because in a world where cyber wars are gaining momentum, caution against situations that could throw institutions into trouble in both legal and practical areas is a crucial issue for both organizations and PR professionals.

This study discusses the topic of data security in the context of cybersecurity from a PR perspective and in relation to data protection. There is a need for qualitative and quantitative studies on this topic. Many studies are conducted based on this information. The future of practical and strategic communication studies is made possible by addressing digital security issues. In this respect, unfamiliar problems await the PR specialists of the future, which need to be solved with significantly more complex and step-by-step applications. This is something that should be borne in mind in future studies.

REFERENCES

"500ŞirketHacklendi". (2015, Ekim 27). *Hürriyet Ekonomi*. Retrieved from Hürriyet Gazetesi: http://www.hurriyet.com.tr/ekonomi/500-sirket-hacklendi-30383340

Akıncı, A. N. (2017). *Avrupa Birliği Genel Veri Koruma Tüzüğü'nün getirdiği yenilikler ve türk hukuku bakımından değerlendirilmesi*. İkdisadi Sektörler ve Koordinasyon Genel Müdürlüğü. T.C. Kalkınma Bakanlığı. Retrieved from http://www.bilgitoplumu.gov.tr/wp-content/uploads/2017/07/AB_Veri_Koruma_Tuzugu.pdf

Aydınlık. (2016, Ekim 4). *Aydınlık Gazetesi*. Retrieved from "Wikileaks tarafından açıklanan 10 büyük sır": https://www.aydinlik.com.tr/wikileaks-tarafindan-aciklanan-10-buyuk-sir

Barnett, M. L., Jermier, J. M., & Lafferty, B. A. (2006). Corporate reputation: The definitional landscape. *Corporate Reputation Review, 9*(1), 26–38.

BGASecurity. (2013). *Gerçek dünyadan siber saldırı örnekleri*. Retrieved from https://www.bgasecurity.com/makale/gercek-dunyadan-siber-saldiri-ornekleri/

Boyd, D., & Hargittai, E. (2010). Facebook privacy settings: Who cares?. *First Monday, 15*(8). Retrieved from http://firstmonday.org/ojs/index.php/fm/article/view/3086

Chun, R. (2005). Corporate reputation: Meaning and measurement. *International Journal of Management Reviews, 7*(2), 91–109.

DeutscheMesse. (2014, April 2). *Hannover Fuarı'nda endüstri 4.0*. Retrieved from deutschland.de: https://www.deutschland.de/tr/topic/ekonomi/kuresellesme-uluslararasi-ticaret/hannover-fuarinda-endustri-40

Dinev, T., & Hart, P. (2005). Internet privacy concerns and social awareness as determinants of intention to transact. *International Journal of Electronic Commerce, 10*(2), 7-29. doi:10.2753/JEC1086-4415100201

Dwyer, C., Hiltz, S. R., & Passerini, K. (2007). Trust and privacy concern within social networking sites: A comparison of facebook and myspace. *13. AMCIS 2007 Proceedings*, (p. 71-110). Keystone: Colorado.

EntegreYazılım. (2018, Mart 25). *Veri Güvenliği*. Retrieved from Entegre Yazılım: https://www.entegreyazilim.com.tr/veri-guvenligi

Eroğlu, Ş. (2018). Dijital yaşamda mahremiyet (Gizlilik) kavramı ve kişisel veriler: Hacettepe Üniversitesi bilgi ve belge yönetimi bölümü öğrencilerinin mahremiyet ve kişisel veri algılarının analizi. *Hacettepe Üniversitesi Edebiyat Fakültesi Dergisi, 35*(2), 130-153. doi:10.32600/huefd.439007

Ersoy, A. R. (Director). (2017). *Endüstri 4.0 (D)evrimi yolunda* [Motion Picture].

Ersöz, B., & Özmen, M. (2020). Dijitalleşme ve bilişim teknolojilerinin çalışanlar üzerindeki etkileri. *AJIT-e: Bilişim Teknolojileri Online Dergisi, 11*(42), 170-179. doi:10.5824/ajite.2020.03.007.x

Goettke, R., & Christiana, J. (2007). Privacy and online social networking websites. in M. D. Smith, J. Waldo, A. Rosen, & A. Friedman, *Computer Science 199r: Special Topics in Computer Science Computation and Society* (pp. 1-13). doi:10.1.1.92.1380

Gotsi, M., & Wilson, A. M. (2001). Corporate reputation: Seeking a definition. *Corporate Communications: An International Journal, 6*(1), 24-30. doi:10.1108/13563280110381189

Govani, T., & Pashley, H. (2014). Student awareness of the privacy implications when using Facebook. *Cyberpsychology, 8*(2), 1-17. Retrieved from http://lorrie.cranor.org/courses/fa05/tubzhlp.pdf

Grunig, J. E., & Hunt, T. (1984). *Managing public relations*. New York: Holt, Rinehart & Winston.

Karakaş, S., Rukancı, F., & Anameriç, H. (2009). *Belge yönetimi ve arşiv terimleri sözlüğü*. Ankara: Devlet Arşivleri Genel Müdürlüğü.

Kaya, C. (2011). Avrupa Birliği veri koruma direktifi ekseninde hassas veriler ve işlenmesi. *İstanbul Üniversitesi Hukuk Fakültesi Mecmuası, 69*(1), 317-334.

Khatri, V., & Brown, C. V. (2010). Designing data governance. *Communications of the ACM, 53*(1), 148–152.

Kovach, S. (2014, September 3). *We still don't have assurance from apple that icloud is safe*. Retrieved from businessinsider.com: https://www.businessinsider.com/apple-statement-on-icloud-hack-2014-9

Langenderfer, J., & Miyazaki, A. D. (2009). Privacy in the information economy. *The Journal of Consumer Affairs*, 380-388.

Ljungqvist, A., & Wilhelm-Jr, W. J. (2003). IPO pricing in the dot-com bubble. *The Journal of Finance, 58*(2), 723–752. Retrieved from http://www.jstor.org/stable/3094556.

Manyika, J., Chui, M., Brown, B., Bughin, J., Dobbs, R., Roxburgh, C., & Hung-Byers, A. (2011). *Big data: The next frontier for innovation, competition, and productivity*. McKinsey Global Institute.

Milliyet. (2011, Haziran 1). *"ABD siber saldırıları 'savaş sebebi' sayacak"*. Retrieved from Milliyet Gazetesi: http://www.milliyet.com.tr/abd-siber-saldirilari-savas-sebebi-sayacak/dunya/dunya-detay/01.06.2011/1397381/default.htm

Miltgen, C. L. (2009). Online consumer privacy concern and willingness to provide personal data on the internet. *International Journal of Networking and Virtual Organizations, Indersciences, 6*(6), 574-603.

Miltgen, C. L., & Peyrat-Guillard, D. (2014). Cultural and generational influences on privacy concerns: A qualitative study in seven European countries. *European Journal of Information Systems, 23*(2), 103-125. doi:10.1057/ejis.2013.17

Newsom, D., Turk, J., & Kruckeberg, D. (2012). *This is PR: The realities of public relations*. Boston MA: Wadsworth Cengage Learning.

NTV. (2011, Haziran 8). Anonymous TİB'e saldırdı! Retrieved from https://www.ntv.com.tr/turkiye/anonymous-tibe-saldirdi,OsGUZ-fEn50SCXCLVyGOIfg

OECD. (2013). *New data for understanding the human condition: International perspectives*. OECD. Retrieved from https://www.oecd.org/sti/inno/new-data-for-understanding-the-human-condition.pdf

Özenç, K. (2007). Bilgi ve iletişim teknolojilerinde kişisel ve kurumsal bilgi güvenliğinin sağlanması. *Uluslararası Katılımlı Bilgi Güvenliği ve Kriptoloji Konferansı*. Ankara.

Özpınar, Ş. B. (2021). Yeni teknolojiler ve kurumsal iletişimin yeni araçları. *Etkileşim, 7*, 150–168.

Öztekin, H., & Öztekin, A. (2010). Modernleşme-mahremiyet ilişikisi ve siber mekanda mahremiyetin aleniyete dönüşmesi. *NWSA: e-Journal of New World Sciences Academy, 5*(4), 526-540.

Paksoy, M. (2012, Ocak 24). *Teknoloji oku*. Retrieved from İlk Siber Silah : Stuxnet !: https://www.teknolojioku.com/guvenlik/ilk-siber-silah-stuxnet-5a28f28f18e540630d1ce10a

Petrov, C. (2022, June 22). *25+ Impressive big data statistics for 2022*. Retrieved from techjury.net: https://techjury.net/blog/big-data-statistics/#gref

Petrovici, M. A. (2014). E-Public relations: Impact and efficiency. *A case study. Procedia-Social and Behavioral Sciences, 141*, 79-84.

PRSSA. (2022, June 20). *Learn about public relations*. Retrieved from prsa.org: https://www.prsa.org/prssa/about-prssa/learn-about-pr

Ridley-Siegert, T. (2015). Data privacy: What the consumer really thinks. *Journal of Direct, Data and Digital Marketing Practice, 17*, 30-35. doi:10.1057/dddmp.2015.40

Silva, B. v., & Larsen, T. (2011). *Setting the watch: Privacy and the ethics of CCTV surveillance*. Hart Publishing.

Sindermann, C., Lachmann, B., Elhai, J. D., & Montag, C. (2021). Personality associations with whatsapp usage and usage of alternative messaging applications to protect one's own data. *Journal of Individual Differences, 42*(4), 167-174. doi:10.1027/1614-0001/a000343

Sophos. (2021). *Sophos 2022 Threat Report: Interrelated threats target an interdependent world*. Sophos ltd. Retrieved from https://assets.sophos.com/X24WTUEQ/at/b739xqx5jg5w9w7p2bpzxg/sophos-2022-threat-report.pdf

Sönmez, H. Ş. (2020). Dijital ortamda yapılan halkla ilişkilerin bir aracı olarak kurumsal bloglar: 2019 yılı türkiye'nin en değerli 25 markası üzerine bir inceleme. *Kocaeli Üniversitesi İletişim Fakültesi Araştırma Dergisi, 16*, 185-207.

Stacks, D. W. (2016). *Primer of public relations research* (Third Edition ed.). New York: Guilford Press.

Symantec. (2013). *Internet security threat report*. Retrieved from http://www.symantec.com/content/en/us/enterprise/other_resources/b-istr_main-_report_v18_2012_21291018.en-us.pdf

Şahinaslan, E., & Şahinaslan, Ö. (2018). E-dönüşüm uygulamalarında güvenlik. *Proceedings of the International Congress on Business and Marketing*, (pp. 420-435).

Şen, F. (2012). Kamu yönetiminde halkla ilişkileri yeniden düşünmek. *Akdeniz İletişim Dergisi, 16*, 63-79.

Tan, Q., & Pivot, F. (2015). Big data privacy: Changing perception of privacy. *2015 IEEE International Conference on Smart City/SocialCom/SustainCom together with DataCom 2015 and SC2 2015*, (pp. 860-865). Retrieved from 10.1109/SmartCity.2015.176

Tanyıldızı, N. İ. (2021). *Dijital dünyada halkla ilişkiler*. Ankara: İksad Yayınevi.

Taşçı, M. E., & Şamlı, R. (2020). Veri madenciliği ile kalp hastalığı teşhisi. *Avrupa Bilim ve Teknoloji Dergisi*(Özel Sayı), 88-95.

Tekerek, M. (2008). Bilgi güvenliği Yönetimi. *KSÜ Fen ve Mühendislik Dergisi, 11*(1), 132.

Tortop, N. (1993). *Halkla ilişkiler*. Ankara: Yargı Yayınları.

Tufan, O. (2017, Ekim 21). *Ddos nedir?*. Retrieved from Shift Delete: https://shiftdelete.net/ddos-nedir

Turney, M. (2015). *Foreshadowing the explanatory and the mutual satisfaction phases of public relations, Ivy Lee was decades ahead of his contemporaries*. Retrieved from Online Readings in Public Relations by Michael Turney: https://www.nku.edu/~turney/prclass/readings/3eras2x.html

Tüfekçi, Z. (2008). Can you see me now? Audience and disclosure regulation in online social network sites. *Bulletin of Science Technology & Society, 28*(1), 20-36. doi:10.1177/0270467607311484

Uğurlu, S. (2018). Dijital PR ve itibar yönetimi açısından sosyal medyada kriz yönetiminde bir vaka incelemesi: "Üsküdar belediyesi - Kedi Evi" projesi. *İnsan & İnsan, 5*(17), 233-248. doi:10.29224/insanveinsan.417128

Vuleta, B. (2021, October 28). *How much data is created every day? [27 Staggering Stats].* Retrieved from SeedScientific.com: https://seedscientific.com/ how-much-data-is-created-every-day/#:~:text=Every%20day%2C%20we%-20create%20roughly%202.5%20quintillion%20bytes%20of%20data.

Wagner, A. E., & Brooke, C. (2007). Wasting time: The mission impossible with respect to technology-oriented security approaches. *Journal of Business Research Methods, 5*(2), 117-124.

Wearesocial. (2022). *Digital 2022 global overview report.* England: We Are Social Ltd.

Weiner, M., & Kochhar, S. (2016). *Irreversible: The public relations big data revolution.* IPR: Institute for Public Relations. Retrieved from https://instituteforpr.org/irreversible-public-relations-big-data-revolution/

Whitten, D., & Leidner, D. (2006). Bringing IT back: An analysis of the decision to backsource or switch vendors. *Decision Sciences, 37*(4), 605–621.

Wiencierz, C., & Röttger, U. (2019). Big data in public relations: A conceptual framework. *Public Relations Journal, 12*(3), 1–15.

Wijoyo, H., Limakrisna, N., & Suryanti, S. (2021). The effect of renewal privacy policy whatsapp to customer behavior. *Insight Management Journal, 1*(2), 26–31.

Wright, D. K., & Hinson, M. D. (2008). How blogs and social media are changing public relations and the way it is practiced. *Public Relations Journal, 2*(2), 1–21.

YeniŞafak. (2017, Kasım 16). *"Apple'ın en güvendiği teknolojinin açığını 10 yaşındaki çocuk buldu".* Retrieved from Yeni Şafak Gazetesi: https://www.yenisafak.com/teknoloji/applein-en-guvendigi-teknolojinin-acigini-10-yasindaki-cocuk-buldu-2810460

Yılmaz, A. (2012). Sosyal medya kullanımında güncel tartışmalar: üniversite öğrencileri örneğinde mahremiyet- kamusal alan ilişkisi. *Global Media Journal, 3*(5), 246-264.

Young, A. L., & Quan-Haase, A. (2013). Privacy protection strategies on Facebook. *Information, Communication & Society, 16*(4), 479-500. doi:10.1080/1369118X.2013.777757

Yüksel, M. (2003). Mahremiyet hakkı ve sosyo - tarihsel gelişimi. *Ankara Üniversitesi SBF Dergisi, 58*(1), 181-213. doi:10.1501/SBFder_0000001619